PERFECT DAY
IOWA

Day Trips, Weekend Getaways, and Other Escapes

Reedy Press
PO Box 5131
St. Louis, MO 63139
www.reedypress.com

Library of Congress Control Number: 2024930398
ISBN: 9781681065250

Title page images courtesy of Sara Broers (left to right): Buddy Holly Crash Site, Clear Lake; Fishback & Stephenson Cider House, Fairfield; Birdsall's Ice Cream, Mason City; French Icarian Village, Corning; If You Build It Exhibit, Dyersville; Lewis & Clark Interpretive Center, Sioux City; Starboard Market, Clear Lake; Grammy Award for Music Man, Mason City

Table of Contents page images courtesy of Sara Broers (left to right): Cedar Valley Arobretum, Waterloo; Backgrounds Coffee Bar & Boutique, Corning; Mural, *Hope Is A Thing with Sequins* by Naomi Haverland, Sioux City; Stone Feather Road, Cedar Falls; Calkins Area Nature Center, Iowa Falls; French Icarian Village, Corning; Background image: Lake Icaria, Corning

Printed in the United States of America
24 25 26 26 27   5 4 3 2 1

Dedication

Dedicated to my grandchildren, James, Jonathan, and Alaina. These three have taught me the importance of slow travel and enjoying every moment.

Beeds Lake State Park, Franklin County
(Courtesy of Sara Broers)

PERFECT DAY
IOWA

Day Trips, Weekend Getaways, and Other Escapes

Sara Broers

Contents

Images courtesy of

Clark Tower, Madison County
(Courtesy of Sara Broers)

Acknowledgments

I am grateful for being a native Iowan. The stories that others share remind me of how lucky I am to call Iowa home. My husband deserves a medal for listening to my Iowa stories. He has heard many. Thank you to my family and everyone who has believed in me and my love of writing. The hospitality that many Iowans have shown me is over the top. Thank you to the many tourism offices across the state that have worked with me over the years; your dedication and hospitality does not go unnoticed.

Arts R Alive, Webster City
(Courtesy of Sara Broers)

Introduction

Iowa is in the heart of America and offers many incredible things to see and do. As a lifelong Iowan, I have learned over the years that we get comfortable in our own backyards, Iowa included. My home state is filled with cities, towns, and counties that each have something special to offer.

When you are looking to spend a perfect day in Iowa, it's easy to do. I have put together a variety of wonderful things to experience. One day in each of these areas is not enough time, as many of them offer more than can be accomplished in 24 hours. I challenge you to experience all 29 of these places. Get to know the people. Yes, there is such a thing as "Iowa nice."

Board the Fenelon Place Elevator in Dubuque, where Iowa started. Walk to the Buddy Holly Crash Site in Clear Lake after touring the legendary Surf Ballroom & Museum, where Holly played his last concert. Visit Stone State Park in Sioux City and overlook the Loess Hills National Scenic Byway, a view unlike any other in the country.

Enjoy your perfect day in Iowa and do what you love to do!

Sara Broers
Mason City, Iowa

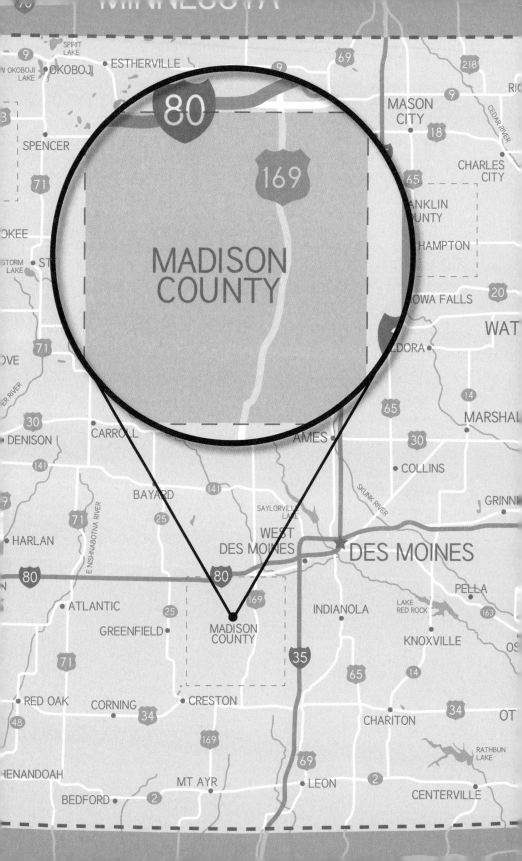

MADISON COUNTY

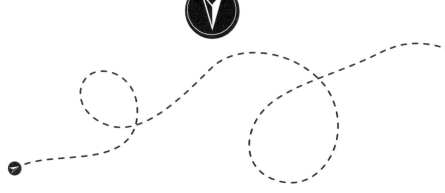

MADISON COUNTY sits in the rolling hills of Central Iowa. It is home to the Covered Bridges of Madison County and well-known actor John Wayne. When you visit Madison County, it is easy to slow down and immerse yourself in small-town America. The Winterset City Park Campground offers a clean, safe place to camp in the heart of Madison County. A unique way to experience this popular Iowa county is to travel to one of the covered bridges after dark has set in. Dark skies are incredible in this area of Iowa, making it a prime location to see the Milky Way and potentially a shooting star. The Winterset Town Square comes to life in the summer months as the large hanging floral baskets dot the square. After visiting the Bakery Unlimited, home of the best apple fritters, shop at the Winterset Town Square. If an ice cream treat is calling your name, Frostee's offers a delicious, cool treat during the warmer months. Embrace all Madison County offers, as you will quickly fall in love.

John Wayne Birthplace & Museum
205 S John Wayne Dr., Winterset
877-462-1044 • johnwaynebirthplace.museum

☑ Located in the charming town of **Winterset**, the memory of John Wayne lives on. Visit the John Wayne Birthplace & Museum. Upon entering the museum, view a documentary on "The Duke's" phenomenal career in the movie theater within the museum. This museum showcases one of Wayne's family cars, a customized 1972 Pontiac Grand Safari station wagon. Movie scripts, letters, artwork, clothing, and John Wayne artifacts—he starred in more than 70 movies through the years, so there's a lot to see. Step into the charming, tiny, four-room home where Wayne was born. As you stroll the grounds, you can feel all the small-town feels that Winterset offers. Tours are self-guided, with staff available to answer your questions. Plan to spend a minimum of an hour at this historical museum. Explore the gift shop and take home John Wayne memorabilia.

John Wayne Museum (Courtesy of Sara Broers)

Covered Bridges of Madison County (Courtesy of Sara Broers)

Covered Bridges of Madison County

73 E Jefferson St., Winterset • 515-462-1187 • madisoncounty.com

Madison County was once upon a time home to 19 covered bridges. Today, there are six bridges—five are listed on the National Register of Historic Places. Roseman, Hogback, and Holliwell Bridges are all on gravel roads. Imes Bridge is in St. Charles, and the Cutler-Donahoe Bridge is at **City Park** in Winterset, the only bridge not listed on the National Register of Historic Places. Both Imes and Cutler-Donahoe bridges are accessible by all paved roads. Cedar Bridge is on a gravel road; if you are traveling from Winterset, it's a few hundred feet of gravel. Cedar Bridge is the only remaining bridge you can drive your vehicle through. Pack a lunch and picnic near one of the beautiful bridges. Fall brings incredible foliage to Madison County, making it a lovely time of year to visit. The **Covered Bridges Scenic Byway** highlights the well-known bridges of Madison County.

Speckled Hen Farms

1578 N River Trl., Winterset • 515-205-4413 • speckledhenfarmsiowa.com

✓ Speckled Hen Farms showcases the rolling hills of Madison County. Kris Miler has created an experience at her farm in rural Madison County. **Friday Nights on the Farm** is a highlight for many, as music sets the tone for all guests. Regular business hours are Sunday from 1 to 4 p.m. Bring a cooler to take home a load of food that you'll not be able to resist sharing with your family. Fresh vegetables are grown on the farm and sold throughout the season. You can shop until you drop by the store that greets all guests upon arrival. Experience local at its finest with local books, crafts, decorations, meats, freshly grown produce, and all things Madison County available to purchase at Speckled Hen Farms.

Speckled Hen Farms (Courtesy of Sara Broers)

Nearby Alternatives

Outdoors: Covered Bridges Scenic Byway

The Covered Bridges Scenic Byway travels an incredible 82-mile-plus route in Madison County. With two wineries, a cidery, and the world-famous Covered Bridges of Madison County, this drive is one to remember. The beautiful **Courthouse Square** in Winterset is a highlight of this route, along with the numerous historical sites of Madison County.

73 E Jefferson St., Winterset
515-462-1185
madisoncounty.com/
covered-bridges-scenic-byway

Museum: Iowa Quilt Museum

The Iowa Quilt Museum sits on the **Town Square** in Winterset. The displays change throughout the year, offering new quilts and experiences for all visitors. Large quilts that are incredible works of art flow through the museum. Unique, colorful patterns and quilts from numerous time periods are featured throughout the museum.

68 E Court Ave., Winterset
515-462-5988
iowaquiltmuseum.org

Unique Lodging: The Roost

The Roost is a beautiful vacation home on **Speckled Hen Farms**'s property. The four bedrooms, beautiful kitchen, and front porch showcase the rolling hills of Madison County. Set your alarm clock for sunrise before you turn in for the night. The spectacular sunrise from the Roost shines in its glory from the front porch.

1578 N River Trl., Winterset
515-205-4413
speckledhenfarmsiowa.com

A Castle Experience: Clark Tower

Winterset City Park boasts a beautiful, 25-foot limestone castle tower. The winding, one-mile gravel road to Clark Tower is a lovely one-way drive. Fall is an incredible time of year to make the trek. Views from the tower overlook the **Middle River Valley** of Madison County.

2278 Clark Tower Rd., Winterset
madisoncounty.com/
clark-tower-2

Trip Planning

Madison County Chamber of Commerce

73 E Jefferson St., Winterset
515-462-1185
madisoncounty.com

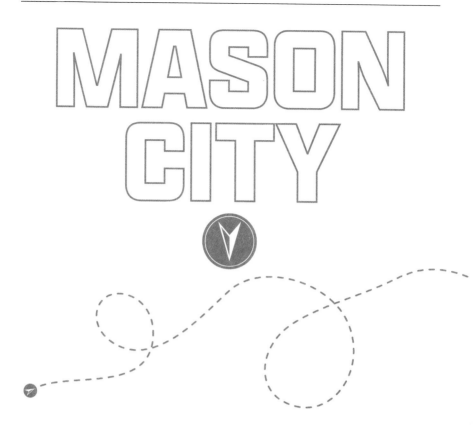

MASON CITY

ARCHITECTURE RULES THE roost in Mason City. It is home to the Historic Park Inn Hotel, the last-known hotel in the world that you can stay at designed by Frank Lloyd Wright. You can experience more architecture through the Stockman House and a walking tour of Wright homes in Mason City. Dine at the award-winning Northwestern Steakhouse and indulge in the best Greek-seasoned steak in the world. Sandwich shops, steak houses, local coffee shops, and brewpubs will keep your taste buds happy.

Birdsall's Ice Cream and the Olde Creamery Ice Cream shops are known for their quality and fun, seasonal flavors. Cannonball Park in East Park is home to the Cannonball 457, the last remaining Minneapolis & St. Louis Railway steam locomotive. Prairie Playground is the largest playground in Mason City and offers a maze of wooden playground equipment for families to enjoy. Many of the attractions in Mason City are walkable, and parking is free throughout the city.

Music Man Square

308 S Pennsylvania Ave. • 641-424-2852 • themusicmansquare.org

✓ Music Man Square features an indoor 1912 Streetscape, which includes an ice cream parlor and gift shop. Set designs from the Warner Bros. motion picture *The Music Man* are located throughout the attraction. An interactive museum boasts memorabilia and music-related exhibits featuring Mason City's Meredith Willson. Willson's birthplace and boyhood home, a restored 1895 modified Queen Anne house, is also on the property. The first Grammy Award from the **National Academy of Recording Arts and Sciences** is in the museum at Music Man Square. Willson was the recipient of the *Music Man* album on May 4, 1959. Two well-known songs that Willson composed are "Seventy-Six Trombones" and "It's Beginning to Look a Lot Like Christmas." Take a selfie with Mason City's Music Man statue, *Meredith Willson*, before leaving the museum complex.

Music Man Square (Courtesy of Sara Broers)

State Street Deli (Courtesy of Visit Mason City)

State Street Deli

107 E State St. • 641-201-1002 • facebook.com/statestreetdeli

A local favorite, State Street Deli, is sure to win you over. This popular sandwich shop in Mason City's Downtown District offers a delightful selection of sandwiches, soups, pastries, and desserts. Grab a quick bite for breakfast at State Street Deli, which offers breakfast sandwiches to kick off your day. The Michigan Avenue Sandwich is a local lunch favorite of smoked turkey, bacon, cheddar, Swiss cheese, and chipotle raspberry mayo on pepper-toasted sourdough bread. Your taste buds will thank you for a sandwich to jump-start your lunch hour. Pair your sandwich with pasta, chips, or potato salad, and you will have the perfect lunchtime meal in **Downtown Mason City**. Save room for a cupcake or two; the dessert case is always packed with deliciousness. The restaurant is a big-city experience in a small town in Iowa.

Charles H. MacNider
Art Museum

303 2nd St. SE • 641-421-3666
macniderart.org

The Charles H. MacNider Art Museum boasts the world's largest collection of Baird's puppets, created by Mason City High School graduate Bill Baird. The display features puppets, marionettes, and other materials collected and made by the famous puppeteer. The beautiful grounds are home to several sculptures of **Mason City's River City Sculptures on Parade** walking tour. Several temporary collections move in and out of the museum annually, making this a reason to visit more than once per year.

The **MacNider Arts Festival** is held annually in June, featuring numerous talented artists and musicians. The museum is free to visit and offers rental space for the perfect birthday party or family events. Stroll the grounds and take time to view the incredible works of art, including *Romare Bearden, George Bellows*, and *Andy Warhol*. The arts are a part of Mason City's culture, and the Charles H. MacNider Art Museum will quickly become a favorite art museum.

Charles H. MacNider Art Museum (Courtesy of Sara Broers)

Nearby Alternatives

Nature Center: Lime Creek Nature Center

Lime Creek Nature Center offers 440 acres of outdoor experiences, including hiking, horseback riding, and mountain biking. Nestled atop the limestone bluffs of the Winnebago River, it's a magical place in North Iowa. The indoor center features wildlife resources and hands-on experiences for families all year long.

3501 Lime Creek Rd.
641-423-5309
mycountyparks.com/county/cerro-gordo/park/lime-creek-nature-center-conservation-area.aspx

Sculpture Tour: River City Sculptures on Parade

City Sculptures on Parade boasts more than 70 sculptures on a 1.9-mile walking tour. Vote for your favorite sculpture between June 1 and September 1. The winning sculpture is purchased by the city of Mason City and becomes a part of the permanent collection. Dress for the season and enjoy the art scene in Mason City.

225 2nd St. SE
641-421-3669
sculpturesonparade.com

Restaurant: Awe'z Sandwich Shop

Iowa's favorite sandwich is the loose meat sandwich; this beef delight is served up with many other favorite Iowa fixings at Awe'z Sandwich Shop in Mason City. Ground beef topped with pickles, onions, and ketchup are the top toppings for lovers of loose meat sandwiches. Grab a malt of your choice, and you have yourself a winning meal.

629 S Federal Ave.
641-424-2662
awezsandwichshop.com

Local Brewpub: Fat Hill Brewing

Fat Hill Brewing is a locally owned-and-operated seven-barrel craft brewery in Downtown Mason City. Their creative beers spotlight locally grown ingredients, including herbs, hops, wildflower honey, and Aronia berries. Live music and events occur all year-round, making this a prime place of enjoyment in Mason City.

17 N Federal Ave.
641-423-0737
fathillbrewing.com

Trip Planning

Visit Mason City

2021 4th St. SW
641-422-1663
visitmasoncityiowa.com

CLEAR LAKE

CLEAR LAKE OFFERS a beautiful 3,684 lakes for enthusiasts. The quaint downtown will lure you in on your first visit. History comes to life at the legendary Surf Ballroom & Museum, where Buddy Holly played his last concert. Travel approximately five miles north of Clear Lake and make the quarter-mile walk to the Buddy Holly Crash Site. The fateful day on February 3, 1959, is the day the music lives.

Clear Lake State Park offers camping, boating, fishing, swimming, and a beach. Book the popular shelter house for your next family reunion; everyone will have something to do. Prominent family-friendly festivals include a 4th of July Celebration, Color the Wind Kite Festival, Winter Dance Party, and the TRI Clear Lake Splash & Dash, to name a few. Grab an ice cream treat at Charlie's Soda Fountain or the Olde Creamery to top off your visit to Clear Lake. An evening ride on the *Lady of the Lake* will capture the spirit of Clear Lake and all it has to offer.

Central Gardens of North Iowa

800 2nd Ave. N • 641-357-0700
centralgardensnorthiowa.com

✓ Clear Lake's Central Gardens of North Iowa offer some of the finest gardens in the Midwest. The gardens are free to visit and offer different events throughout the season. More than 20 unique-themed gardens offer something for everyone. Two acres offer tranquility and peace that you will only find here. There's something to be said about colorful flowers and butterfly gardens.

The **Stream Garden** is one of the most popular themed areas in the garden. Upon entering, grab a book at the **Little Free Library**, kick back, and read a book while listening to the peace in the gardens. Several events occur throughout the season from Fresh on Fridays to the **Summer Garden Party & Auctions**. With 90 percent of the work done in the gardens by volunteers, this is one of North Iowa's best-kept secrets. The gardens are a short walk from the **Downtown Seawall**, making it a nice stroll from the Downtown Clear Lake area.

Central Gardens of North Iowa (Courtesy of Sara Broers)

Starboard Market (Courtesy of Starboard Market)

Starboard Market

310 Main Ave. • 641-357-0660 • facebook.com/starboardmarket

✔ If you are looking for a sandwich that you will be talking about for years on end, look no further than Starboard Market. This popular Iowa eatery offers dozens of sandwiches, and you are sure to find the perfect one. If sandwiches are not your thing, try the homemade salads, including potato salad, like your grandma used to make. Your meal must be topped off with an Iowa Scotcheroo, pumpkin bar, the best mint brownie you will have in your lifetime, or a sugar cookie that will melt in your mouth. Everything at Starboard Market is made with old-fashioned love in the kitchen, including stirring, mixing, baking, and serving up the tastiest lunch menu in the Midwest. For a memorable lunch in Clear Lake, enjoy your meal in Clear Lake Central Park, a one-block walk from the restaurant. Get in line at 11 a.m. and be there before 2 p.m. Starboard Market closes at 2 p.m. (ish), so plan accordingly.

Surf Ballroom & Museum

460 N Shore Dr. • 641-357-6151 • surfballroom.com

The legendary Surf Ballroom & Museum is a must-experience for anyone passionate about music. Musical artists from all over the world have performed in the Surf Ballroom. The Winter Dance Party is held annually, celebrating the life of Buddy Holly, Ritchie Valens, and the Big Bopper. The narrative of the history of this iconic venue is also told through the many photographs of performers and their memorabilia on display. Visit the "green room" to see if you can find the signature of your favorite musical artist.

On September 6, 2011, the Surf Ballroom & Museum was added to the National Register of Historic Places. Today, you can sit in one of the original booths when attending an event at the Surf Ballroom. During your visit, don't miss the guitars that many artists have signed and left after playing on the stage at this historic Iowa cultural icon.

Surf Ballroom & Museum
(Courtesy of Sara Broers)

Nearby Alternatives

Outdoors: Clear Lake State Park

Clear Lake State Park features 50 acres of recreational opportunities, featuring mature oak trees and a popular campground. Many who visit this Iowa state park enjoy picnicking, boating, fishing, and kayaking. A historic lodge is available for rent.

6490 S Shore Dr.
641-357-4212
iowadnr.gov/places-to-go/
state-parks/iowa-state-parks/
clear-lake-state-park

Music History: Buddy Holly Crash Site

On February 3, 1959, American musician Buddy Holly perished in a plane crash north of Clear Lake. Today, visitors make the quarter-mile hike to the Buddy Holly Crash Site. The iconic Buddy Holly glasses greet you as you begin your trek. Please be respectful as this is located on private property.

22728 Gull Ave.
641-357-2159
clearlakeiowa.com/how-to-visit-
the-buddy-holly-crash-site

Shopping: Louie's Custom Meats & More

Louie's Custom Meats & More will not disappoint. If you are staying in a vacation home in the area, shop for delicious meats and all the sides. A proud member of the Iowa Cattlemen's Association, Louie's specializes in Black Angus beef, natural pork, and free-range and fresh chicken, all cut to order. Don't miss their baked goods on Saturdays, including donuts and banana bread. But those are only offered while supplies last; Louie and his team say, "It's worth the drive!"

810 US Hwy. 18 W
641-357-6100
louiescustommeats.net

Restaurant: Cabin Coffee Co.

Cabin Coffee was founded in Clear Lake in 2002 for locals and tourists to enjoy their coffees, pastries, and sandwiches in a comfortable setting on Main Avenue. From lattes to espressos, as their motto states, "Just be happy and have fun." Cabin Coffee has become an Iowa staple with locations throughout the state and region.

303 Main Ave.
641-357-6500
cabincoffeecompany.com

Trip Planning

Clear Lake Area Chamber of Commerce

205 Main Ave.
641-357-2159
clearlakeiowa.com

SIOUX CITY

SIOUX CITY IS in an area that encompasses Iowa, Nebraska, and South Dakota. With more than 70 miles of recreational trails, the outdoor experiences are endless. Live theater, concerts, and music festivals are all popular events throughout the year. The historic Orpheum Theatre, a performing arts center, is home to the Sioux City Symphony Orchestra. History comes to life through several museums and experiences throughout the Siouxland Region.

Experience a Twin Bing at Palmer's Olde Tyme Candy Shoppe and Jolly Time Pop Corn at Koated Kernels, locally produced favorites. Sioux City pride shines throughout the community. Stroll the historic walking district and look upward to view the new murals popping up. Experience all four seasons in Sioux City. The Loess Hills National Scenic Byway begins north of Sioux City and travels through the area. Stone State Park offers an incredible view of the byway. Explore Sioux City with an eagerness to see new things, and I guarantee that you will have a delightful day in Sioux City.

Sioux City Railroad Museum

3400 Sioux River Rd., IA Hwy. 12 N · Loess Hills Scenic Byway
712-233-6996 · siouxcityrailroadmuseum.org

✓ The Sioux City Railroad Museum offers 32 acres to stroll through all things related to the railroad. Admission is free for all visitors. The Nebraska Central Model Railroad exhibit is just one of the eye-catching displays. The 75-foot-by-15-foot HO-scale (rail transport modeling scale) model railway came from the Durham Museum in Omaha. Its permanent home is in the Civil Engineering Hall at the Sioux City Railroad Museum. The room is filled with several railroad exhibits throughout the complex. If you have young kids, the numerous model railroad exhibits will keep them entertained for hours.

On weekends, the "Sioux City & Dakota Railroad" gives train rides for 32 passengers. One of the railcars is ADA accessible, making this an attraction for everyone. Several railroad models will inspire and remind you of the love of railroads in America. A recent addition is the "Holocaust Rails Expedition," which takes visitors back to World War II and the horrors of the Holocaust. The railcars on display showcase how people from the Sioux City area were impacted by the Holocaust with firsthand accounts from survivors.

Sioux City Railroad Museum
(Courtesy of Sara Broers)

Dorothy Pecaut Nature Center (Courtesy of Sara Broers)

Dorothy Pecaut Nature Center

4500 Sioux River Rd. • 712-258-0838
woodburyparks.org/dorothy-pecaut-nature-center

✓ Nature lovers will appreciate all that the Dorothy Pecaut Nature Center offers. Located in the Loess Hills of Iowa, the incredible views that Lewis and Clark most likely experienced are situated within the nature center. The well-maintained hiking trails offer fantastic hiking for all family members. An indoor museum starts your visit, and then you can venture outdoors. Inquire at the information desk to learn about trail closures or pertinent information for your visit. Wildlife, including deer and turkey, are abundant. Dress in layers, wear a good pair of hiking shoes, and carry a pair of binoculars. This year-round nature center offers unique experiences for Iowa's four seasons. Look up and around as the 150-year-old giant oak trees will greet you everywhere you go. Birding enthusiasts will appreciate the views, as well as the butterfly gardens that are surrounded by wildflowers. Youngsters will want to enroll in Iowa's Junior Naturalist Program, as it's a fun way to experience highlights of Iowa's nature.

Marto Brewing Company

930 4th St. • 712-226-BEER • martobrewing.com

☑ Located on Historic Fourth Street in Sioux City, the Marto Brewing Company is a brewery and gathering place with an atmosphere that is just welcoming and fun. Your server will have a smile and make sure you have a great experience. Beers, appetizers, unique and locally sourced meals, and amazing desserts—this place has you covered. During the warmer months, grab a table in the outdoor dining area. The outdoor dining season always seems short in the Midwest, so enjoy it while you can. Paninis are a popular quick lunch item, and their Neapolitan pizzas and wood-fired pasta are popular items any time of the day. Sunday brunch is served from 10 a.m. to 2 p.m. featuring andouille sausage and eggs and biscuits and gravy. Enjoy a taste of the area by ordering the "Loess Hills," featuring three eggs cooked the way you like with your choice of four strips of bacon or one house-made sausage, served with whole-wheat toast. I don't know about you, but I'm now hungry for brunch!

Marto Brewing Company (Courtesy of Sara Broers)

Nearby Alternatives

Outdoors: Stone State Park
Stone State Park, on the Loess Hills National Scenic Byway, has more than 15 miles of hiking trails. The incredible views overlooking the scenic byway are unmatched. View the fall colors from one of the park's overlooks. Pack a picnic lunch and surround yourself with nature, as Stone State Park will lure you in.
5001 Talbot Rd.
712-255-4698
iowadnr.gov/places-to-go/state-parks/iowa-state-parks/stone-state-park

Museum: Lewis and Clark Interpretive Center
Permanent and temporary exhibits tell the Siouxland leg of the Lewis and Clark Expedition at the Lewis and Clark Interpretive Center. Video and moving and speaking animatronic figures bring the story to life. Plan to spend at least two hours exploring this gem in the area.
900 Larsen Park Rd.
712-224-5242
siouxcitylcic.com

Restaurant: The Diving Elk
The Diving Elk serves up classic cocktails, craft beer, and quality food in a friendly atmosphere. Enjoy Sioux City's Historic Fourth Street with friends and a memorable meal. From flatbread to poutine, your taste buds will thank you. And yes, the restaurant is named after "The Famous Diving Elks." In the early 1900s, W. H. Barnes of Sioux City was fascinated by the way elk jumped, from five feet to twenty feet.
1101 4th St.
712-234-0000
facebook.com/thedivingelk

Hotel: Hard Rock Hotel & Casino Sioux City
Calling all music fans! With more than 640 slot machines and 18 table games, the Hard Rock Hotel & Casino will entertain you for hours. Book a night's stay at the Hard Rock Hotel and enjoy this boutique, 54-room property in Downtown Sioux City.
111 3rd St.
712-226-7600
hardrockcasinosiouxcity.com

Trip Planning
Explore Sioux City

119 4th St., Ste. 104
712-224-1000
exploresiouxcity.org

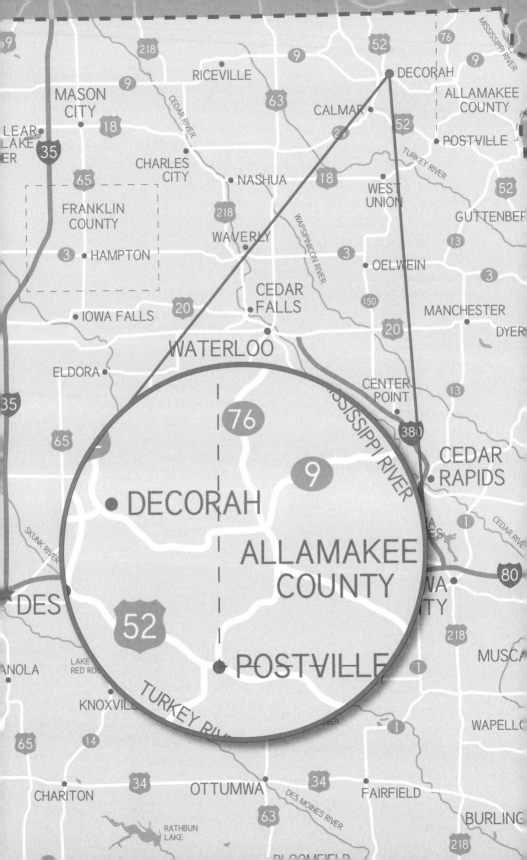

DECORAH

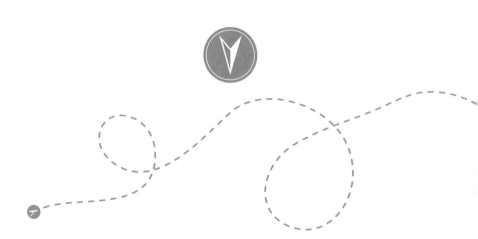

DECORAH IS IN the Driftless area of Northeast Iowa. The glaciers skipped Decorah and the surrounding area, leaving it with valleys, hills, rivers, and limestone bluffs to enjoy. The outdoor experiences are numerous. There's an outdoor adventure for everyone, from kayaking, biking, canoeing, and fly-fishing. With multiple trout streams in the area, you will have success tossing in a line here and there. The quaint downtown area will win you over in a heartbeat. Everything is walkable, and staying at historic Hotel Winneshiek will top off your Decorah experience. Mabe's Pizza, a pizzeria downtown, has been in business for 70 years. You can never go wrong with a slice of taco pizza from Mabe's. Fresh food is important to the area. Many restaurants purchase local food at the Decorah Farmers Market vendors. Nordic Fest is a famous weekend festival held annually in Decorah. The traditions and culture of Norway are celebrated during the last weekend in July. From lefse to colorful crafts and a Saturday night fireworks display, you will quickly become a Norwegian for a day in Decorah.

Toppling Goliath Brewing Company

1600 Prosperity Rd. • 563-387-6700 • tgbrews.com

☑ Toppling Goliath Brewing Company is consistently recognized nationwide as one of the best breweries in the Midwest and beyond. Grab an on-tap beer or bring in the family for a meal. Beers on tap include the Luther Lager, a fruity beer. This blueberry lager is named after the local college and features the crisp, clean taste of Dorothy's New World Lager with Cascade hops and blueberry juice. The taco pizza and sandwiches will quickly win everyone over at your party. During the warmer months, sit outdoors and enjoy the live music. Toppling Goliath Brewing Company is not only a brewpub and restaurant, but it's also a gathering place for the locals and people from the region. This popular Decorah brewpub has become a destination experience in its own way.

Toppling Goliath Brewing Company (Courtesy of Sara Broers)

Trout Run Trail (Courtesy of Sara Broers)

Trout Run Trail

mycountyparks.com/county/winneshiek/park/trout-run-trail.aspx

☑ The Trout Run Trail is an 11-mile paved trail that runs around Decorah. People of all ages enjoy this popular trail—walkers, bicyclists, and runners can be seen at all hours of the day. The **Decorah Fish Hatchery** sits alongside the trail and makes for a perfect stop. If you are biking with kids, they will enjoy the fish. Be sure to bring quarters to buy food to feed the fish. The trail winds around the Upper Iowa River, offering scenic views throughout your time there. A short stop off the trail is the **Whippy Dip**, offering soft-serve ice cream that will melt your taste buds on a hot summer day. Several picnic tables along the trail offer opportunities for a relaxing picnic spot. The twists and turns of the trail's path are sure to bring smiles to your face as you explore nature on the Trout Run Trail.

Pinter's Gardens & Pumpkins

2475 State Hwy. 9 • 563-382-0010
pintersgardensandpumpkins.com

Pinters Gardens & Pumpkins is a sprawling "agri-tainment" spot that jumps for joy in the fall. Families come from all around to experience fall in the Pumpkin Patch, and all that it has to offer. The Pumpkin Patch offers wagon rides, a large jumping pillow, big slides, and a corn maze, providing hours of entertainment for all family members. Another fall highlight is picking the best apples for your baking and eating needs in their apple orchard. The bakery features cupcakes of all varieties, popcorn, homemade fudge, cookies, turnovers, and cinnamon rolls. The flavors and variety of baked goods change often, giving you good reason to swing in for a return visit. Spring is a prime time to invest in new plants, landscaping, and fruit trees. The garden center is sure to help you keep your yard looking fresh. Make a full day at Pinter's Gardens & Pumpkins; your family will thank you for the memories.

Pinter's Gardens & Pumpkins (Courtesy of Sara Broers)

Nearby Alternatives

Museum: Vesterheim Norwegian-American Museum

The Vesterheim Norwegian-American Museum features a world-class collection of 33,000 artifacts and a heritage park of 12 historic buildings. A folk art school offers free events throughout the year. Take home a taste of Norway in Decorah by visiting their gift shop and stocking up on folk art supplies and gifts.

520 W Water St.
563-382-9681
vesterheim.org

Outdoors: Dunning's Spring Park

Dunning's Spring Park is home to a beautiful scenic overlook over the waterfall in the park. Decorah's Ice Cave is believed to be the largest known ice cave in eastern North America. Spring, summer, and fall are the best seasons to visit.

Ice Cave Rd.
563-382-4158
parks.decorahia.org/
decorah-parks

Restaurant: Whippy Dip

The Whippy Dip is the place to be in Decorah in the warmer months of the year. There's nothing like a nice scoop of soft-serve ice cream—or malts, shakes, parfaits, and sundaes. For a change of pace, order a dipped cone in a flavor of your choice.

111 College Dr.
563-382-4591
facebook.com/whippydip52101

Farmers Market: Decorah Farmers Market

The Decorah Farmers Market showcases local food and goods from Northeast Iowa's small producers and artisans. This market moves indoors in November and December, keeping local produce available most of the year.

Heivly St.
563-382-3990
visitdecorah.com/farmers-market

Trip Planning

Visit Decorah

507 W Water St.
563-382-3990
visitdecorah.com

CEDAR FALLS

CEDAR FALLS IS in Cedar Valley, home to the University of Northern Iowa. With a college campus in town, there's no shortage of sporting activities. History comes to life in Cedar Falls through the Victorian Home and Carriage House Museum and the Ice House Museum. With more than 130 miles of hard-surfaced trails, soft trails, and miles of paddling trails, adventure is everywhere. Two national trails are in the Cedar Valley: the American Discovery Trail and the Great American Rail Trail. If you have ever wanted to visit all seven local craft breweries and taprooms in Cedar Falls, a Beer Trail Passport is calling your name. The local food scene offers many options, from fine dining to a casual dining experience. Gilmore's Pub is a popular hangout featuring locally sourced foods, including a perfect 10-ounce New York strip. No matter how you spend your day, you will enjoy all that Cedar Falls offers.

Tony's La Pizzeria

407 Main St. • 319-277-8669 • facebook.com/tonyslapizzeria

✓ Tony's La Pizzeria started out as a simple pizza shop in 1958. It is the second-oldest pizzeria in the Cedar Falls/Waterloo area. Its current location on Main Street is a prime spot to find both high-quality pizza and service. The pizza dough is made on-site daily. The Iowa-grown pork and sausage are ground every week. The milk, cream, and ice cream come from **Hansen's Dairy** in Hudson, a local dairy farm. You are guaranteed a homemade and locally sourced pizza at Tony's, which is not common in today's world. Of course, pizza is a top menu item, but there are several other options. The homemade sausage sandwich or a barbecue chicken sandwich will have you telling everyone about your meal at Tony's La Pizzeria in Cedar Falls.

Tony's La Pizzeria (Courtesy of Sara Broers)

Hartman Reserve Nature Center (Courtesy of Sara Broers)

Hartman Reserve Nature Center

657 Reserve Dr. • 319-277-2187
hartmanreserve.org

✓ The Hartman Reserve Nature Center is a 300-plus-acre nature reserve in Cedar Falls. It is in an urban area, but you are deep in nature once you get into the park. The nature center is home to displays that will inspire you to dig deep into nature. The Hartman Reserve is a designated **Watchable Wildlife (IA DNR) Monarch Waystation (Monarch Watch)** and important **Bird Area (National Audubon Society)**. The monarchs and birding experiences are second to none. When you explore the trails in the Hartman Reserve Nature Center, ensure your smartphone is with you. You can scan the QR codes at the trail markers. You will not only experience the beauty of nature, but you will also learn a little something along the way. There are varied levels of hiking trails, so pay attention to the signage. If you are an experienced hiker, you can take to any of the trails without issues. The trails are open from sunrise to sunset, but the nature center has set hours.

Tip: The restroom on the south side of the building is open daily from sunrise to sunset.

Cedar Falls's Main Street

310 E 4th St. • 319-277-0213 • communitymainstreet.org

✓ Cedar Falls's Main Street is a mecca of architecture and art. In 1987, several concerned citizens formed Community Main Street, Inc. This dedicated group realized the importance of having a healthy Main Street in Cedar Falls. Today, several beautiful sculptures on Main Street are unique to Cedar Falls. From decorations for your home and/or business to serious coffee shops, there is a shop on Main Street that you will want to frequent. The **Black Hawk Hotel** is a 28-room boutique hotel, the second-longest-operating hotel in the United States. Stay in a historic hotel on Main Street, and you can walk to everything you want to see and do in Cedar Falls. No matter where you choose to spend your time in the Downtown District in Cedar Falls, you will find something that interests you—and likely make you want to return over and over.

Sculpture on Cedar Falls's Main Street (Courtesy of Sara Broers)

Nearby Alternatives

Museum: Cedar Falls Historical Society

The Cedar Falls Historical Society is made up of five experiences: the **Victorian House Museum, Ice House Museum, Little Red Schoolhouse, Lenoir Model Train**, and the **Behrens-Rapp Filling Station**. Each of these experiences offers visitors different ways to dig deeper into Cedar Falls's history.

308 W 3rd St.
319-266-5149
www.cfhistory.org

Restaurant: The Cedar Falls Brown Bottle

The Cedar Falls Brown Bottle has served delicious Italian food for your special night out for over 50 years. Memories have been made here as a destination restaurant for family night or date night. Fresh, local, and homemade are the key ingredients for their long-term success.

1111 Center St.
319-266-2616
thebrownbottle.com

Outdoors: Disc Golf at Tourist Park

Disc Golf at Tourist Park is an 18-hole course in Cedar Falls. If you are a novice, experienced, or someone who just wants to check out the sport of disc golf, this is an excellent course for you. The experience is free; bring three golf discs to play. With three discs, you will be assured you have one to toss. It's not uncommon to lose one here and there. I speak from experience on this.

400 Center St.
319-273-8636
cedarfalls.com/215/tourist-park

Shopping: Stone Feathered Road

Stone Feathered Road is a higher-end clothing and accessories boutique on Main Street. With classic and timeless pieces, along with trendy looks, you will surely find your look at Stone Feathered Road. Highly influenced by the "Lifestyle West," they offer custom-made jewelry and bags, one-of-a-kind items, unique apparel, and outerwear. They also have the largest cowhide selection in Northeast Iowa.

218 Main St.
319-260-2050
stonefeatherroad.com

Trip Planning

Cedar Falls Tourism
6510 Hudson Rd.
319-268-4266
cedarfallstourism.org

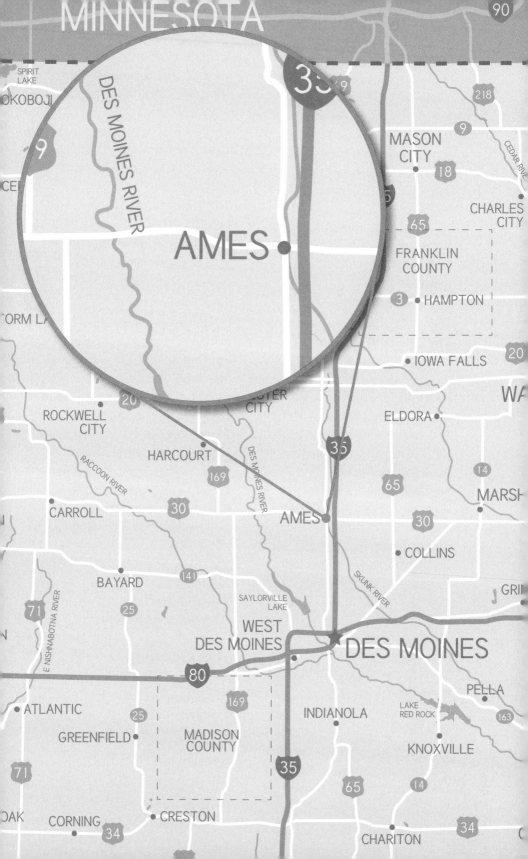

AMES

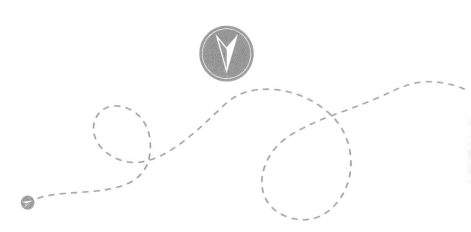

AMES IS IN the heart of Iowa, a short 30-minute drive north of Des Moines. It is a regional hub for central Iowa. With a growing population, Ames is attractive to many types of people. Iowa State University was established in 1858 and attracts a diverse population. When you stroll Ames's Historic Main Street, you will feel the slower pace that will take you back to a quieter place in time. The shopping scene is huge in Ames, so come prepared to enjoy food, coffee shops, and fun restaurants all around. Game day is always bustling in Ames at Iowa State University. If you find yourself in need of Iowa State apparel, Moorman Clothiers can come to your rescue. Are European chocolates calling your name? The Chocolaterie Stam offers unique chocolate and coffees. You can either shop till you drop or take things nice and slow in Ames. It's up to you as to how you spend your perfect day.

Reiman Gardens

1407 University Blvd. • 515-294-2710 • reimangardens.com

Reiman Gardens, on the Iowa State University campus, is home to 17 acres of year-round attractions featuring indoor and outdoor gardens. **The Conservatory** hosts seasonal displays throughout the year. With numerous butterflies flying throughout, it's possible they may land on you. Check to make sure you don't exit with a butterfly on you or on your belongings. A children's garden showcases Iowa's agricultural heritage, with a maze, tumbling mounds, butterfly bench, and so much more. Elwood, the World's Largest Concrete Gnome, lives at Reiman Gardens, so be sure to take a selfie when you find him. Holidays offer something new at the gardens, including a massive holiday light experience. Plan to spend an hour or a full day strolling, relaxing, and sipping on a lemonade or hot cocoa while enjoying the beautiful Reiman Gardens.

Reiman Gardens (Courtesy of Sara Broers)

Historic Main Street (Courtesy of Sara Broers)

Ames's Historic Main Street
304 Main St. • 515-233-3472 • amesdowntown.org

☑ Historic Ames's Main Street became nationally recognized when it was listed on the National Register of Historic Places in 2019. Stroll at your own pace and experience the sculptures that dot the blocks that are filled with restaurants, bars, unique shopping experiences, and art galleries. **Dog-Eared Books** is a bookstore that caters to anyone who loves books and reading. **The Pumpkin Patch Gallery** offers children's clothing, books, and unique, hard-to-find toys. Quilt enthusiasts will appreciate the Quilting Connection, a shop that offers fabric, quilting kits, and gift ideas. There's something for everyone in the more than 50 shops that line Ames's Historic Main Street. Many shops carry Iowa State gear, ensuring you have the proper red and gold to wear to Iowa State events. Shop 365 days of the year and experience the fun Main Street experience that Ames has to offer.

Dublin Bay Irish Pub & Grill

320 S 16th St. • 515-956-3580 • dublinbayames.com

✓ Dublin Bay Irish Pub & Grill is a classic Irish pub featuring old-wood decor, craft beers, a traditional Irish menu, and an outdoor patio. The baked potato soup is always comforting and delicious. Order a Guinness barbecue burger featuring a half-pound fresh burger with Guinness barbecue sauce and all the burger fixings. Classic bangers and mash will give you all the feels of Ireland while dining in Iowa. This classic dish features Irish sausages on garlic mashed potatoes with onion gravy and sautéed red onions, along with red and green peppers. A side of buttered peas will round out your classic Irish meal. Shepherd's pie in savory beef gravy topped with toasted mashed potatoes is a great option for people looking for a gluten-free Irish meal. Even if you are not Irish, become an Irishman for a day while enjoying a delicious meal in Ames.

Tip: Order the delicious, mouthwatering bread pudding for dessert.

Dublin Bay Irish Pub & Grill (Courtesy of Dublin Bay Irish Pub & Grill)

Nearby Alternatives

Restaurant: Sweet Caroline's Kitchen and Cocktails Bar and Restaurant

Sweet Caroline's Kitchen and Cocktails Bar and Restaurant serves up homestyle cooking done right. Caroline's famous fried chicken and cheese curds are local favorites, accompanied by a craft cocktail. Arrive hungry and allow yourself plenty of time to enjoy the full menu.

316 Main St.
515-802-4105
sweetcarolinesames.com

Outdoors: Ada Hayden Heritage Park

Although Ada Hayden Heritage Park is in an urban location, it is a complete outdoor landscape for birding, fishing, hiking, and cross-country skiing in season. Kiddos are sure to enjoy the wide, paved bike paths. If you are looking for solitude and peace surrounded by nature, this is your park!

5205 Grand Ave.
515-239-5101
cityofames.org/home/
components/facilitydirectory/
facilitydirectory/2/471?seldept=13

Shopping: Dog-Eared Books

Dog-Eared Books, one of Iowa's most popular bookstores, is a destination experience located within Ames's Historic Main Street. Join a book club or participate in the Writers Lab. Experience culture, network with others, and learn a few things along the way at Dog-Eared Books.

203 Main St.
515-598-7508
dogearedbooksames.com

Sporting Event: Jack Trice Stadium

Although sporting events happen all year round at Iowa State University, plan your perfect fall day around a football game at Jack Trice Stadium. You will quickly become an Iowa State fan for a day, or potentially a lifetime, with 55,000 fans.

1732 Jack Trice Way
515-294-5527
cyclones.com/index.aspx

Trip Planning

Discover Ames

1601 Golden Aspen Dr.
Ste. 110
515-232-4032
discoverames.com

O'BRIEN COUNTY

O'BRIEN COUNTY SITS in Northwest Iowa and is home to 14,000 residents. O'Brien County has numerous outdoor experiences, including the Glacial Trail Scenic Byway. A highlight of the scenic byway is the Prairie Heritage Center. Did you know that you can sleep in a grain bin and a Carnegie Library in O'Brien County? The Sheldon Recreational Trail offers six miles of asphalt for bikers, hikers, and in-line skaters during the warmer months. With 10 parks throughout the county, you will find one that meets your needs. Yesterday's Memories car and truck museum in Sanborn offers thousands of items to take you down memory lane. A handful of antique shops dot the county for antiques enthusiasts. Harley, Paulina, Sanborn, Sheldon, and Sutherland all have antique shops waiting for you. Solsma's Pumpkin Patch and Fireworks is in its 24th year. Summertime features fireworks, and fall features a large pumpkin patch and corn maze. No matter where you spend your time in O'Brien County, you will have the time of your life.

Prairie Heritage Center

4931 Yellow Ave., Peterson • 712-295-7200 • prairieheritagecenter.org

☑ Prairie Heritage Center sits on Iowa's **Glacial Trail Scenic Byway** near Peterson. This nature center is surrounded by Iowa prairie lands and offers educational experiences. Walking into the nature center, you will spy a pair of binoculars near the windows. Grab them and look out the window to the prairie; birding is popular in this area of Iowa. Summertime brings incredible color as the wildflowers are in full bloom. There are several hiking trails, with the longest trail being a little more than one mile. View the covered wagon and climb the tower to view the prairie. The bison roam freely in the fenced area next to the tower. Bring a picnic lunch to enjoy on the prairie. The Prairie Heritage Center is a great option if it rains, as several incredible displays are indoors. This nature center will not disappoint; it has many stories to tell.

Prairie Heritage Center (Courtesy of Sara Broers)

JW's Bar and Grill (Courtesy of Sara Broers)

JW's Bar and Grill | 117 N Main St., Paullina • 712-949-2525
facebook.com/p/jws-bar-grill-100057676680934

☑ JWS Bar and Grill in Paullina offers home-cooked food made with love. JW's Bar and Grill is your go-to restaurant for broasted chicken. Although broasted chicken takes a little longer to cook, it's always well worth the wait. Dine in or order your family-size chicken dinner with all the fixings to go. Your chicken dinner includes coleslaw, potato salad, broasted potatoes, and cottage cheese. Specialty sandwiches include the Big Wilbur, a 10-ounce burger topped with bacon, cheese slices, and an onion ring served on Texas toast. Are you hungry yet? A variety of kid's meals include chicken strips, corn dogs, macaroni and cheese, grilled cheese, hamburgers, and cheeseburgers. And if you want a classic Iowa meal, order the grilled pork chop. Everyone here loves anything pork!

Dog Creek Park

4901 Warbler Ave., Sutherland • 712-295-7200
mycountyparks.com/county/obrien/park/dog-creek-park.aspx

☑ Dog Creek Park, along the **Glacial Trail Scenic Byway** near Sutherland, offers 29 campsites, two camping cabins, and two grain bin cabins. That's right; you can book a stay in a grain bin at Dog Creek Park! This is one of the most unique lodging experiences in Iowa. These grain bins have queen beds, electricity, a full kitchen, cable television, Wi-Fi, and a handicap-accessible bathroom with a walk-in shower. Twelve people can comfortably stay in one of the grain bins. You are surrounded by nature and can enjoy a beautiful dark-sky adventure when the sun sets. Dog Creek Park offers kayaking and canoeing. Manual and battery-operated boats are allowed on the water. Relax and connect with nature while having the amenities of home at Dog Creek Park.

Dog Creek Park (Courtesy of Sara Broers)

Nearby Alternatives

Arts Center: Prairie Arts Historical Park

The Prairie Arts Historical Park in Sheldon features an 1870 pioneer home, four country schools, a house where ceramics are created. Kids can become a budding Picasso with kids art classes. Create ceramic masterpieces and spend time in a building full of O'Brien County history.

1423 Park St., Sheldon
712-324-9718
facebook.com/prairieartscouncil

Restaurant: Jay's Restaurant and Lounge

Jay's Restaurant and Lounge in Sanborn has been family owned for over 70 years. Enjoy this family-friendly restaurant for breakfast, lunch, and dinner, serving local specialties and timeless favorites. The house-specialty prime rib is served with special seasonings and slow-cooked to perfection. Make sure to order a trip to Jay's colossal soup and salad bar!

120 W 7th St., Sanborn
712-930-3886
jaysinsanborn.com

Museum: Yesterday's Memories & Truck Museum

Yesterday's Memories & Truck Museum in Sanborn houses thousands of items from years gone by. The Vander Haag family continues to share their collection of cars, trucks, children's toys, fuel pumps, and the like. Plan to spend a minimum of three hours exploring the museum's treasures.

106 Eastern Ave., Sanborn
712-729-3268
yesterdaysmemories.us

Outdoors: Sheldon City Park

The Sheldon City Park is home to a playground paradise, a large wooden castle for kids to climb and adventure through. Softball fields, picnic tables, grills, and a covered gazebo make this a destination park for family reunions.

Between 4th and 6th Aves., South of Hwy. 18, Sheldon
712-324-4651
sheldoniowa.gov/pages/parks-rec-pool

Trip Planning

Tour O'Brien County

160 S Hayes Ave., Primghar
712-957-1313
tourobriencounty.org

PELLA

PELLA IS A short, 50-minute drive from Des Moines, Iowa's capital. Pella is known as America's Dutch Treasure. You can visit North America's largest working windmill and Wyatt Earp's boyhood home in one stop. The sweet treats and pastries are some of the best in the state. Dutch bakeries, meat shops, and a family-owned chocolate shop make Pella the perfect place for foodie experiences. The annual Tulip Festival in May attracts visitors from all around the world. Dutch heritage is celebrated all season long, making it a festival to remember. Christmas brings the annual Kerstmarkt, Pella's Dutch Christmas Market, bringing people together to celebrate the upcoming Christmas season. No matter what time of year you visit, Pella is an extraordinary town of fewer than 12,000 residents. Birding is popular in the surrounding area, along with several parks. Lake Red Rock, Iowa's largest lake, offers outstanding water activities nearby. Exploring Pella will be a memorable day as smiles abound.

VanVeen Chocolates

613 Franklin St. • 641-780-9374 • vanveenchocolates.com

An out-of-this-world chocolate shop awaits you in Pella. VanVeen Chocolates is a family-owned chocolate shop in the heart of Pella offering beautiful homemade chocolates. Sea salt caramel chocolates are a fan favorite. If chocolate-covered cherries are your thing, they also have you covered. If chocolates are not calling your name, cotton candy of all flavors is also available for purchase. Assorted gift boxes are popular throughout the year. During Tulip Time, Pella's annual tulip festival, VanVeen Chocolates will have unique colorful tulips and flowers for you to enjoy. From the artsy homemade chocolates to the "classic" candies, you are sure to find them in this quaint chocolate shop that sits on the main drag in Pella. If you find yourself home and realize you missed out on the chocolates in Pella, reach out to the owners of VanVeen Chocolates, and they will be happy to arrange a delivery.

Van Veen Chocolates (Courtesy of Sara Broers)

Historical Village (Courtesy of Sara Broers)

Pella Historical Village and Vermeer Windmill

507 Franklin St. • 641-620-9463
pellahistorical.org

The Pella Historical Village and Vermeer Windmill are in the same museum complex in Pella. The Vermeer Windmill is one of the tallest working windmills in North America. It was brought in 2002 from the Netherlands. It was disassembled to ship to Pella and reassembled. Tours of the windmill take you five floors up, showing you where grain came into the windmill and to the top floor where grain is milled. Step onto the deck for an epic view of Pella above Main Street's skyline. The historical village showcases sod houses, along with blacksmithing. When you visit this museum complex, you will learn about the Scholte family, Pella's founding family. You can also see where Wyatt Earp lived and experience Dutch culture to its finest for a perfect day in Pella.

Lake Red Rock

1105 N Hwy. T-15 • 641-828-7522 • recreation.gov/camping/gateways/160

☑ Lake Red Rock is home to Iowa's largest lake. Boaters, campers, bikers, fishermen, bird enthusiasts, and anyone loving the outdoors will enjoy Lake Red Rock. Northern pike, walleye, white bass, and channel catfish are popular in Lake Red Rock. Hop on your bicycle and explore the 17-mile **Volksweg Trail** connecting Pella to Lake Red Rock. If you are biking with kids, a playground is along the trail to break up your bike ride. No matter the season, the beauty of the Lake Red Rock area shines brightly. Summer brings green; fall brings all the yellows, reds, and oranges; and winter brings white! Bald eagles love the Red Rock Lake area in the winter, making bald eagle watching a great travel experience. Everyone enjoys spring as the spring colors burst after a long, white winter. Picnicking is popular along Lake Red Rock, as there are several places where you can set up a picnic with a view of the lake. With 12 campgrounds and day-use facilities, campers will enjoy camping near and around Lake Red Rock.

Lake Red Rock Trail (Courtesy of Sara Broers)

Nearby Alternatives

Restaurant: In't Veld's Meat Market

Enjoy homemade Pella bologna at In't Veld's Meat Market, along with award-winning beef jerky. Grab one of their butcher's boxed lunches at the deli and walk across the street to **Central Park** to enjoy a complete lunch. Their hot and cold sandwiches, wraps, sides, and soups are a reason why they were named a 2021 Iowa Tourism Award winner.
820 Main St.
641-628-3440
intvelds.com

Historical Landmark: Pella Opera House

The Pella Opera House was Pella's first four-story structure in the heart of downtown Pella. The most recent remodel was completed in 2016. Listed on the National Register of Historic Places, enjoy concerts, meetings, reunions, and other events held in this lovely, historic venue.
611 Franklin St.
641-628-8625
pellaoperahouse.org

Shopping: Silver Lining

There's always a Silver Lining; this Silver Lining just happens to be where you can also find good things in small packages. Unique gifts, treasures, and the like are just waiting to be found. Stroll through this charming shop on Main Street and enjoy a perfect shopping day in Pella.
637 Franklin St.
641-780-3836
silverliningpella.com

Bakery: Jaarsma Bakery

Anytime you visit Pella, you need to enjoy a Dutch specialty pastry. The Dutch letter has an addictive, moist almond paste filling in this S-shaped puff pastry. Candies, cakes, breads, and other treats all homemade in Pella will showcase a delicious taste of Holland.
727 Franklin St.
641-628-2940
jaarsmabakery.com

Trip Planning

Visit Pella
915 Broadway St.
641-204-0885
visitpella.com

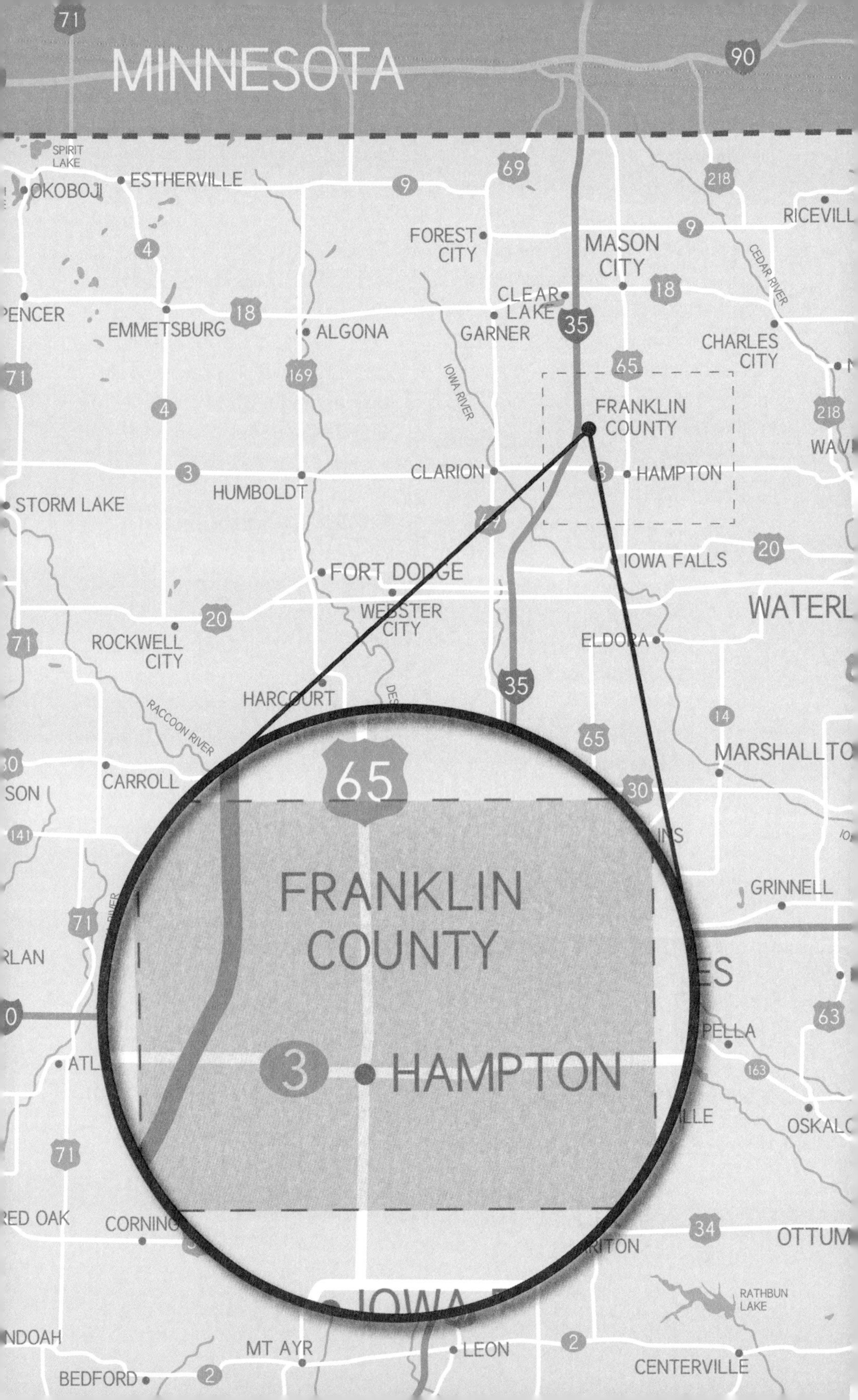
MINNESOTA
SPIRIT LAKE
OKOBOJI
ESTHERVILLE
FOREST CITY
MASON CITY
RICEVILL
CEDAR RIVER
CLEAR LAKE
GARNER
EMMETSBURG
ALGONA
CHARLES CITY
IOWA RIVER
FRANKLIN COUNTY
CLARION
HAMPTON
HUMBOLDT
STORM LAKE
IOWA FALLS
FORT DODGE
WEBSTER CITY
WATERL
ROCKWELL CITY
ELDORA
HARCOURT
RACCOON RIVER
MARSHALLTO
CARROLL
GRINNELL
FRANKLIN COUNTY
HAMPTON
PELLA
OSKALO
CORNING
OTTUM
RATHBUN LAKE
MT AYR
LEON
BEDFORD
CENTERVILLE

FRANKLIN COUNTY

FRANKLIN COUNTY IS in North Central Iowa and offers incredible shopping and spectacular outdoor adventures. Iowa experiences all four distinct seasons, so you'll find things to keep you busy all year. Maynes Grove, south of Hampton, offers outdoor adventures throughout the year. Beeds Lake State Park is where campers enjoy the lake and the ability to kick back and relax in a family-friendly campground. Both outdoor parks offer beautiful hiking experiences for hikers of all levels. Coffee shops, eateries, jewelry, and gift shops are abundant on Hampton's Main Street. History runs deep in Franklin County, as the Soldiers Memorial Hall honors 44 men who died in the American Civil War. This is the only building built to honor Civil War soldiers west of the Mississippi River. Coulter is home to the Franklin County, Iowa, Freedom Rock, a tribute to veterans and their families. No matter how you spend your time in Franklin County, you will wish you had more time to linger.

Maynes Grove

946 US Hwy. 65, Hampton • 641-456-4375
mycountyparks.com/county/franklin/park/maynes-grove.aspx

☑ Maynes Grove is five miles south of Hampton on the Historic Jefferson Highway, US Highway 65. With 250-acres of multiuse recreation, Maynes Grove offers horseback riding, biking, and hiking. Maynes Grove's four-season lodge is a highlight. With 1,600 square feet and a full kitchen, this park is a fantastic place to host an event. With two ponds on-site, canoeing and kayaking are popular. The small ponds are an excellent place for beginners to learn. Fishing for bluegill, catfish, sunfish, and bass is also popular for families. The shoreline and dock are both family friendly. The list of things to do at Maynes Grove continues with picnicking. Two areas are specified for picnics, but you can easily enjoy a picnic throughout the park when you bring your favorite chairs. July brings incredible colors to the restored prairie, where you will want to spend hours. No matter how you spend your day at Maynes Grove, or during which season, you will enjoy all it offers.

Maynes Grove (Courtesy of Sara Broers)

Rustic Brew (Courtesy of Sara Broers)

Rustic Brew

117 1st St. NW, Hampton • 641-456-2141 • facebook.com/rusticbrewhampton

Rustic Brew is where the locals hang out to kick off their day. It's common to find a table of friends discussing "life" with a cup of coffee in hand. You will see an extensive menu of drink options when you set foot inside the doors. Choose whatever is calling your name for the day. Freshly roasted coffees, craft beers, and wine are highlights. Sandwiches, soups, and homemade comfort foods are on the menu. Fun, unique Iowa items can be found throughout the restaurant on the walls loaded with fun decor. The atmosphere creates a vibe authentic to Rustic Brew; you will not find it anywhere else. Dine solo with a friend or a large group; you will feel welcome at the Rustic Brew in Hampton.

Harriman-Nielsen Historic Farm

23 10th St. NW, Hampton • 641-456-5777
fchsiowa.org/harriman-nielsen-historic-farm

☑ Franklin County prides itself on history. Hampton's Harriman-Nielsen Historic Farm, on the National Register of Historic Places, allows visitors to peek into the history of Franklin County. Dr. Oscar Bryan Harriman came to Franklin County from the East Coast in the 1800s. He was a resident of Hampton from 1865 through 1905. Dr. Harriman invested his time and money in the development of the town. He owned the local newspaper and opera house and helped develop the downtown area. He and his family lived on the 45-acre property now known as the Harriman-Nielsen Historic Farm. The house is the lone remaining original building on the property. The **annual fall festival** is when the farm comes to life with tractor rides, pumpkins, music, carnival games for kids, and other demonstrations. No matter when you visit, stroll through the farm and imagine what life was like long ago.

Harriman-Nielsen Historic Farm (Courtesy of Sara Broers)

Nearby Alternatives
Restaurant: God Fuel
A healthy, energizing meal is what you will find at God Fuel in Hampton. The Mediterranean bowl is popular with the locals. You can never go wrong with a taco, but make them chipotle, Hawaiian, lime-cilantro, or Mediterranean.
703 Central Ave. W, Hampton
641-531-9656
god-fuel-llc.square.site

Outdoors: Beeds Lake State Park
Beeds Lake State Park, northwest of Hampton, offers camping, hiking, fishing, and a family-oriented beach. Hike down to the waters of **Spring Creek** below the dam for a beautiful view of the dam and creek.
1422 165th St., Hampton
641-456-2047
iowadnr.gov/places-to-go/
state-parks/iowa-state-parks/
beeds-lake-state-park

Shopping: The Wood Cellar
The Wood Cellar in Hampton is a charming Main Street shop with all the decor you could possibly need for your home. This specialty shop will keep your home looking fresh, new, and ready to greet the following season.
8 1st St. NW, Hampton
641-456-5510
facebook.com/thewoodcellar

Museum: Franklin County Historical Museum
The Franklin County Historical Museum is open by appointment and boasts several unique displays. Franklin County Native Bob Artley's work is showcased in the museum. He was a well-known author, cartoonist, and illustrator.
1000 Central Ave. W, Hampton
641-456-5777
fchsiowa.org/historical-museum

Trip Planning
Franklin County Tourism and Chamber Office
5 1st St. SW, Hampton
641-456-5668
hamptoniowa.org

DES MOINES

IOWA'S CAPITAL CITY, Des Moines, and the surrounding communities offer big amenities in an affordable area of the country. Des Moines is centrally located, with something going on all the time. Des Moines's metro area is spread out, so you never feel like you are in a city of 730,000 people. The food scene is outstanding, with farm-to-table experiences featuring Iowa-grown beef, eggs, and fresh produce. If breweries and distilleries are your passion, Des Moines will not disappoint, as they offer indoor and outdoor spaces. Families will appreciate family-friendly spectator events and outdoor spaces for family participation. The art scene is strong in Des Moines, featuring the Pappajohn Sculpture Park. Iowa's State Capitol Building's 23-karat golden dome towers over the skyline. Lauridsen Skatepark, the country's largest skate park, is in the heart of downtown Des Moines. No matter how you spend your time in Des Moines, you will have the most perfect day ever.

Living History Farms

11121 Hickman Rd., Urbandale • 515-278-5286 • lhf.org

Living History Farms offers 500 acres of storytelling. With more than 300 years of history, there's a lot of storytelling to be told. The story of Midwestern agriculture and rural life is showcased throughout this attraction. You can visit the **1700 Iowa Indian Farm, 1850 Pioneer Farm, 1875 Town, 1900 Horse-Powered Farm**, and the modern **Exhibit Center**. Stroll the grounds at your own pace, on your own time. On-site interpreters are happy to answer your questions and show you how things are done in the world of agriculture. There's always something new to see at Living History Farms. The seasons change as the crops grow. All three of the museum's working farm sites are completely accessible to all guests. Tickets can be purchased at the door. If you are attending a special event, purchasing tickets ahead of the event is recommended.

Tip: There is a lot of walking at this attraction. Wear good walking shoes and carry water with you.

Living History Farms (Courtesy of Living History Farms)

Iowa State Capitol (Courtesy of Sara Broers)

Iowa State Capitol Building

1007 E Grand Ave. • 515-281-5591 • www.legis.iowa.gov/resources/tourcapitol

✔ The Iowa State Capitol Building is a magnificent building in the **East Village** neighborhood of Des Moines. Its Renaissance Revival style and 275-foot gold-leaf dome make it stand out. This is the only five-domed capitol building in the United States. It towers above the skyline, and if you are traveling on the east side of the downtown area, you will see it through your car's windshield. Tours are given throughout the day at no cost, lasting approximately 90 minutes. All groups are encouraged to call 515-281-5591 for the tour schedule on the given days. Tour guides do their best to accommodate every tour request. Inside the capitol building, you will see many works of art, marble fixtures, and wood and stone carvings. Stroll the grounds outdoors around the Iowa State Capitol Building to see different sculptures and memorials.

The Big Steer

1715 Adventureland Dr., Altoona • 515-967-6933 • thebigsteerrestaurant.com

☑ Are you looking for an outstanding prime rib? Look no further than the Big Steer in Altoona. The all-American meat menu showcases Iowa's finest prime rib or beef with a rib eye, filet, porterhouse, filet tips, New York strip, sirloin, or an Italian steak. If you are not hungry for steak, choose a French dip sandwich, barbecue ribs, or a lobster tail. Leave room for dessert! The Heath Bar triple chocolate cake is well worth the wait. No matter the season, you will have a delightful meal at the Big Steer. Come hungry and indulge in all that this amazing menu has to offer. The menu is extensive, and the "supper club"–like environment is one you will appreciate. Have an event coming up? The Big Steer offers catering services as well.

The Big Steer (Courtesy of the Big Steer)

Nearby Alternatives

Gardens: Greater Des Moines Botanical Garden

The Greater Des Moines Botanical Garden offers several garden spaces for you to indulge in the scent, beauty, and experience. This attraction is accessible to all, and there is an elevator for everyone to access the domed conservatory's balcony.

909 Robert D. Ray Dr.
515-323-6290
dmbotanicalgarden.com

Restaurant: Smitty's Tenderloins Shop

Smitty's Tenderloins Shop is home to an award-winning Iowa pork tenderloin. This local eatery will win you over after your first bite. Belly up on a barstool and have yourself an outstanding meal. A milkshake or sundae will top off your meal.

1401 Army Post Rd.
515-287-4742
smittystenderloin.com

Outdoors: Neal Smith National Wildlife Refuge

The Neal Smith National Wildlife Refuge is a short drive from Des Moines in Prairie City. Drive the five-mile auto tour that tells the story of the native tallgrass prairie heritage. View the bison through the windshield of your car. Make sure to save enough time to explore the incredible indoor displays before you depart the refuge.

9981 Pacific St., Prairie City
515-994-3400
fws.gov/refuge/neal-smith

Entertainment: Ironside Axe Club

The Ironside Axe Club is a venue where you can relax, unwind, and throw an axe or two. The community at this club will welcome you and invite you to embrace your Viking spirit. Ironside Axe Club is a great place to start if you are new to axe throwing, as the staff is very accommodating.

2700 University Ave., #100
West Des Moines
515-630-0319
ironsideaxeclub.com

Trip Planning

Catch Des Moines

400 Locust St., Ste. 265
800-451-2625
catchdesmoines.com

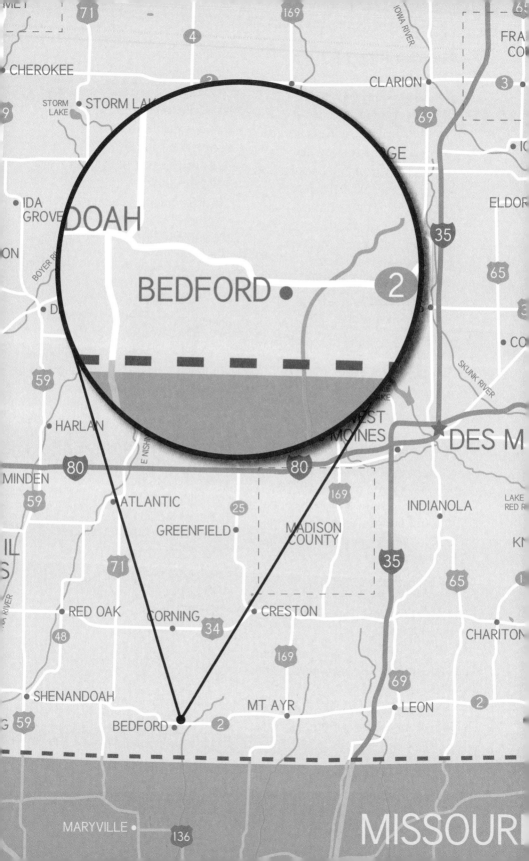

BEDFORD

BEDFORD IS A small, charming town in Southern Iowa. The historic downtown area offers historic buildings with unique architecture. The iconic red bricks will catch your eye. The shops downtown offer books, children's toys, home decor, and special gifts for others. Outdoor activities are numerous with Lake of Three Fires State Park nearby. The Bedford Golf Club offers golf and other community activities, like trivia nights. History comes to life at the Taylor County Museum. Discover the indoor displays and explore the outdoor experiences. This small museum in Bedford will surprise you. Local eateries pride themselves on home-cooked meals, giving you an opportunity to enjoy dining with the locals. The energy on Main Street in Bedford will surprise you. This small, rural town is busting at the seams. Slow down and enjoy all that Bedford has to offer.

Lake of Three Fires State Park

2303 Lake Rd. • 712-523-2700 • iowadnr.gov/places-to-go/state-parks/iowa-state-parks/lake-of-three-fires-state-park

☑ Lake of Three Fires State Park is a hot spot for equestrian trail riding and camping. The diverse outdoor recreation opportunities are endless. The 85-acre lake is popular with boaters and anglers. It's important to note that boats must be operated at a "no-wake" speed. Two boat ramps provide convenient access to the water. Fishermen catch bluegill, crappie, channel catfish, and largemouth bass. More than 10 miles of trails wind around the lake, making it a popular spot for hiking enthusiasts. Snowmobiling is popular on the multiuse trail in the winter months. Two modern campgrounds and an equestrian campground with five holding pens are on-site. Six modern camping cabins are reservable all year long. Each cabin has heat, air conditioning, a refrigerator, a microwave, and a cooktop stove. Enjoy Lake of Three Fires State Park and make memories relaxing around the beautiful lake.

Lake of Three Fires State Park (Courtesy of Sara Broers)

Junction Cafe (Courtesy of Sara Broers)

Junction Cafe

804 Pollock Blvd. • 712-523-2454

✔ Calling all strawberry fans: Order the strawberry shortcake at the Junction Cafe in Bedford for a meal to remember. Breakfast consists of everything you could want for a homemade breakfast, including a pancake that will drape off your plate. If biscuits and gravy are calling, enjoy a plate of this breakfast classic. By tossing on some black pepper, you will have the best biscuits and gravy in Southern Iowa. If you enjoy biscuits on the sweeter side, top it with a pat of butter and warm maple syrup for a winning breakfast. People travel from miles around to enjoy this little café in Bedford. Funnel fries are a hot commodity; order them any time of year and you will feel like you are at the county fair. Deep-fried batter and powdered sugar? Yes, please. Indulge in a Junction burger, a hamburger topped with your favorite toppings. No matter what you are hungry for, Junction Cafe has you covered. Oh, and did I tell you they cook up a killer hot beef sandwich? The hardest part of dining at Junction Cafe is choosing what you want to order!

Hedgie's Books, Toys & More

416 Main St. • 712-523-2371
shophedgies.com

✓ Hedgie's Books, Toys & More is not only a destination bookstore, but is also an award-winning gift shop. In 2018, Hedgie's won Southwest Iowa's Favorite Gift Shop award. Hedgie's is all about customer service. This bookstore caters to you, the customer. They want to be sure they carry the books that you want. If you need a book shipped across the country, they are happy to provide that service. Hedgie's is part of Bedford's beautiful architectural buildings on Main Street. I loved seeing that this locally owned bookstore also carries local food products. When the local folks in Southwest Iowa have an incredible product, Hedgie's is not afraid to stock it. You will find flavored coffee, Iowa wines, and other locally made food items. Local events in the bookstore draw in people from all across the Southwest Iowa region, along with the Omaha area. Visit once, and I guarantee you that you will be back.

Hedgie's Books, Toys & More (Courtesy of Sara Broers)

Nearby Alternatives

Museum: Taylor County Museum

The Taylor County Museum is a gem located in Bedford. Indoor displays include one-room schoolhouses and heirloom quilts. Outdoor experiences include a round barn as well as an actual log cabin from early in Taylor County's history. This well-kept historical museum is clean, inviting, and is free to visit. Donations are accepted.

1001 Pollock Blvd.
712-523-2041
taylorcomuseum.wixsite.com/taylorco

Restaurant: Tampico Family Mexican Restaurant

The flashy, colorful artwork in Tampico Family Mexican Restaurant will instantly put a smile on your face. Order your favorite tacos, including shrimp tacos. For a change of pace, order the Mexican pizza. Top it with your choice of meat and the typical fixings.

413 Main St.
712-427-9040
tampicomexicanrestaurant.org

Shopping: Be Still Mercantile

Be Still Mercantile, on Main Street in Bedford, sells all things Iowa. Products include Iowa home decor, Iowa furniture, Iowa-grown popcorn, Iowa-themed specialty gifts, and everything in between. Be prepared to leave with a few Iowa gifts for yourself and others.

405 Main St.
712-303-7095
facebook.com/
bestillcreationsbedfordia

Outdoors: Bibbins Park

With 20 acres of rolling hills and Burr Oak trees, Bibbins Park offers a place to explore the outdoors. Three playgrounds, a basketball court, a croquet court, a fishing pond, and several shelter houses make this park a great place to spend time with others.

Grant St. and State St.
712-523-2210
bedfordia.org/pview.
aspx?id=4058&catID=147

Trip Planning

Bedford Area Chamber of Commerce
305 E Main St.
540-586-9401
bedfordareachamber.com

FAIRFIELD

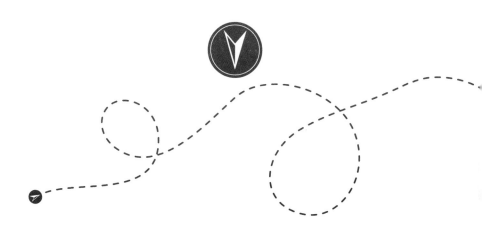

FAIRFIELD SITS IN Southeastern Iowa and has a vibe that you will only find there. You will immediately sense the calmness that the community has to offer. The downtown area is filled with shops that offer feel-good experiences and a sense of community. Scarlett & Co. offers candle-making and fun local products—what an exceptional way to enjoy a night out with girlfriends! When was the last time you dined on tacos for breakfast? Dine at Taco Dreams for a memorable breakfast. Radiance Dairy Farm, an organic, grass-based dairy, provides unique products to the community. People travel many miles to purchase milk, whipping cream, yogurt, and cheese. Their products are found in three grocery stores and approximately 20 restaurants in Fairfield. The esteemed Maharishi International University plays into the vibe of Fairfield, encouraging meditation and relaxation. Once you visit this diverse community, you will feel the Fairfield Vibe.

Maharishi Vedic Observatory

1973 Grand Ave. • 641-472-6344
facebook.com/fortmuseumfv

This unique, one-and-one-half-acre, open-air observatory is comprised of sundial-like instruments that measure the sun. These sundials count the hours of the day, reflecting the movement of the sun, planets, and stars across the sky. When you look at each unique sundial, you will see a shadow giving you the time of day. As you open the fence to enter this unique Iowa attraction, you will sense that the laws of nature are present. You may experience a new connection through the planets and stars. The Maharishi Vedic Observatory is an experimental town of Vedic City, part of the **Maharishi International University** that is a short drive from the observatory. Stroll through this unique attraction and let the vibe sink in. As you leave, you will have a sense of peace and relaxation.

Maharishi Vedic Observatory (Courtesy of Sara Broers)

Jefferson County Heritage Museum (Courtesy of Sara Broers)

Jefferson County Heritage Museum

112 S Court St. • 641-472-6343
jeffersoncountyheritage.org

☑ The Jefferson County Heritage Museum is an Iowa treasure listed on the National Register of Historic Places. The **Carnegie Historical Museum** is located on the first and third floors of the former Fairfield Public Library. It was the first Carnegie library west of the Mississippi River, endowed by Andrew Carnegie. The collections date back to 1876, making it one of Iowa's five oldest museums. Fairfield's history is exhibited on the first floor and provides a fantastic overview of the community. It should be of no surprise that class reunions visit this venue when they are in town. Native American artifacts, Parsons College memorabilia, Civil War and Lincoln artifacts, and pioneer tools and firearms are all displayed in the museum. Birding is showcased within the museum with an extensive bird exhibit. A display of "Fairfield birds" showcases species observed within three miles of town by Mr. and Mrs. William G. Ross between 1901 and 1904. Birding is as popular today as it was in the early 1900s.

Due South

102 N 2nd St. • 641-233-6112

☑ Due South is the combination of two well-known restaurants in Fairfield. The Broth Lab and The Lunchbox combined in early 2024. Chef Camp serves up a combination of the flavors of SouthEast Asia and Southern comfort food under one roof. His Alabama roots are strong in his delicious dishes as he continues adding surprising flavors to the food served at Due South. You can expect to enjoy sandwiches that delight your palate, including the banh mi, a classic Vietnamese sandwich on a ciabatta roll. Plant based burgers, colorful salads, and flatbreads are popular lunch options. Sunday brunch, lunch or dinner out with your soulmate are all good reasons to experience the flavors that this incredible Fairfield restaurant has to offer. The deliciousness of Due South will be an experience you talk about with all of your friends, it's that good!

Due South (Courtesy of Sara Broers)

Nearby Alternatives

Outdoors: Birding at Cedar Creek Trail

Fairfield is home to incredible birding with local birding enthusiasts Michael and Diane Porter. Bring your binoculars and dress for the weather as you stroll the 4.3 miles through the Cedar Creek Trail. The trail is level and easy to walk. The trail is free to use, and it is open all year round.

visitfairfieldiowa.com/events/
bird-hike-along-cedar-view-trail

Restaurant: Fishback & Stephenson Cider House

The award-winning Fishback & Stephenson Cider House offers hard cider and one of the best burgers in the state of Iowa. The beef served is pasture-raised for the best flavors and cuts of meat. Dine with friends and enjoy the amazing view of Iowa heaven.

1949 Pleasant Plain Rd.
641-451-7726
fscider.com

Dairy Tour: Radiance Dairy

Schedule a tour at Radiance Dairy and get to know a local Fairfield farmer. Pet a cow and learn how this local organic, sustainable, grass-fed dairy operation works. The Fairfield vibe shines on through this dairy farm. There are few places in the country where you can get up close with a cow.

1745 Brookville Rd.
641-472-8554
facebook.com/radiancedairy

Museum: ICON Iowa Contemporary Art

The ICON Iowa Contemporary Art Museum is home to the Anonymous Shiva Linga Paintings Hudson Collection. Several exhibitions come and go, giving you a reason to visit repeatedly. Find a seat in the gallery and let the Fairfield vibe sink in.

58 N Main St.
641-919-6252
icon-art.org

Trip Planning

Fairfield Convention & Visitors Bureau

200 N Main
641-472-2828
visitfairfieldiowa.com

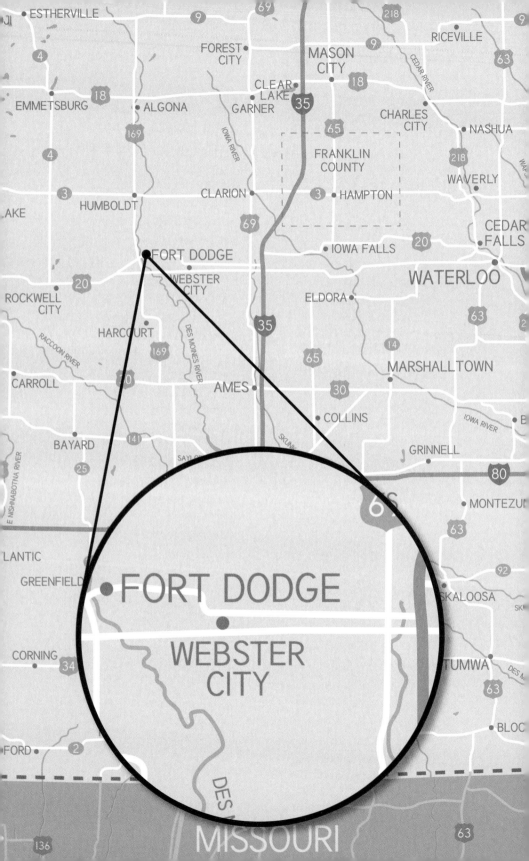

FORT DODGE

FORT DODGE IS home to Iowa's tallest mural, which towers over 100 feet. From history to outdoor adventure, Fort Dodge has something for everyone. Of course, the town would not be named Fort Dodge if it did not have a fort. The Fort Museum & Frontier Village is an excellent place to begin your day in Fort Dodge. Mountain bikers, kayakers, horseback riders, and hiking enthusiasts will appreciate all that this Iowa town offers. Wineries and brewpubs continue to thrive, with events scheduled throughout the year. You can dine on Mexican, American, and Korean food any day of the week in Fort Dodge. Gaga & Hoo brings people across the Midwest to dine on their fine Korean food experience. A fun seasonal experience is visiting the Community Orchard, which offers everything to do with apples. No matter when you visit Fort Dodge, you will be pleasantly surprised at everything that will make you say, "I had no idea this was in Fort Dodge."

Tea Thyme

2021 6th Ave. S • 515-576-2202 • teathymeatsadies.com

✓ Tea Thyme is an upscale, friendly dining experience in Fort Dodge. When you visit, you can expect to see ladies wearing red hats, farmers wearing bib overalls, and everything in between. Lunch is served from 11 a.m. to 2 p.m., and reservations are recommended. Coffee, tea, and dessert are served from 2 p.m. to 4 p.m. The menu changes throughout the year with seasonal offerings. You can always count on a delicious chicken salad croissant or any salad. Norwegian meatballs and chicken and bacon pasta occasionally appear on the menu. My fall favorite is the caramel apple cider, accompanied by a slice of pie. Another terrific dessert choice is anything with a puff pastry. Plan to make Tea Thyme a lunch choice in Fort Dodge. This is one meal you will be talking about for months on end.

Tea Thyme (Courtesy of Sara Broers)

The Community Orchard (Courtesy of Sara Broers)

The Community Orchard

2237 160th St. • 515-573-8212 • communityorchard.com

☑ The Community Orchard is a seasonal business that draws people in from many areas. Denny and Emily Stucky purchased this thriving orchard in May 2022, continuing the orchard's traditions over the years. The **Apple Orchard Cafe** is open from August through December for lunch. Scarecrow Soup is a fan favorite, along with classic sandwiches such as the apple picker sandwich. Dessert must be an apple pie, warm apple dumpling, fresh apple turnover, or an apple streusel muffin. When you visit an apple orchard, it's only appropriate to order as many apple desserts as possible. There's always something going on, from family movie nights to the annual sunflower festival. The **Back 40 Playground** features farm games, duck races, a farm tile slide, and more. Plan to spend a whole day at the Community Orchard for an epic experience.

Fort Museum & Frontier Village

| 1 Museum Rd. • 515-573-4231 |
| fortmuseumfv.com |

✓ History comes to life at the Fort Museum & Frontier Village. Celebrate Fort Dodge's history from the mid-1800s through recent years through the museum and village. The replica stockade and frontier village feature a one-room schoolhouse and an original 1850s log cabin home. Events are held throughout the year, giving you a reason to visit at different times. Stroll through the buildings on-site and experience what life was like in simpler times. The buildings have been well maintained, and most are handicap accessible. Plan for a minimum of a two-hour visit. You can easily spend half a day exploring this historical site in Fort Dodge. Dress for the weather, as the buildings are outdoors, and you will walk between them. If you have questions about any of the displays, ask the employees on the grounds, and they will be happy to answer.

Fort Museum & Frontier Village (Courtesy of Sara Broers)

Nearby Alternatives

Outdoors: Dolliver Memorial State Park

Dolliver Memorial State Park is a short 20-minute drive from Fort Dodge. It offers high bluffs and ravines within the Des Moines River Valley. Two family cabins and a campground are available for lodging. Hiking, kayaking, canoeing, and boating are popular activities in Dolliver Memorial State Park.

2757 Dolliver Park Ave., Lehigh
515-359-2539
iowadnr.gov/places-to-go/
state-parks/iowa-state-parks/
dolliver-memorial-state-park

Restaurant: Gaga & Hoo

Gaga & Hoo provides the best Korean meal experience in Iowa. The bulgogi (Korean beef barbecue) and galbi (Korean short ribs) are local favorites. Family-sized meals are available, along with a variety of drinks. A side dish of yellow pickled radish, rice, or kimchi will round out your meal.

368 Country Club Dr.
515-302-9765
gaga-hoo.com

Public Art: Guido van Helten Silo Mural

Iowa's tallest mural, the 110-foot-tall Fort Dodge Grain Silo Mural, was created by Australian artist Guido van Helten. The 360-degree masterpiece showcases residents of Fort Dodge. When you stand at the base of this mural, you will quickly be lured into the detail that went into this painting.

722 Hawkeye Ave.
888-573-4282
fortdodgepublicart.org/fort-
dodge-grain-silo-project-histo

Museum: Blanden Memorial Art Museum

The Blanden Art Museum has several permanent art collections, including modern American and European paintings, African sculptures, and glassworks. Numerous events and art classes are held throughout the year, offering everyone an opportunity to learn.

920 3rd Ave. S
515-573-2316
blanden.org

Trip Planning:

Visit Fort Dodge

24 N 9th St., Ste. C
888-573-4282
dodgetheordinary.com

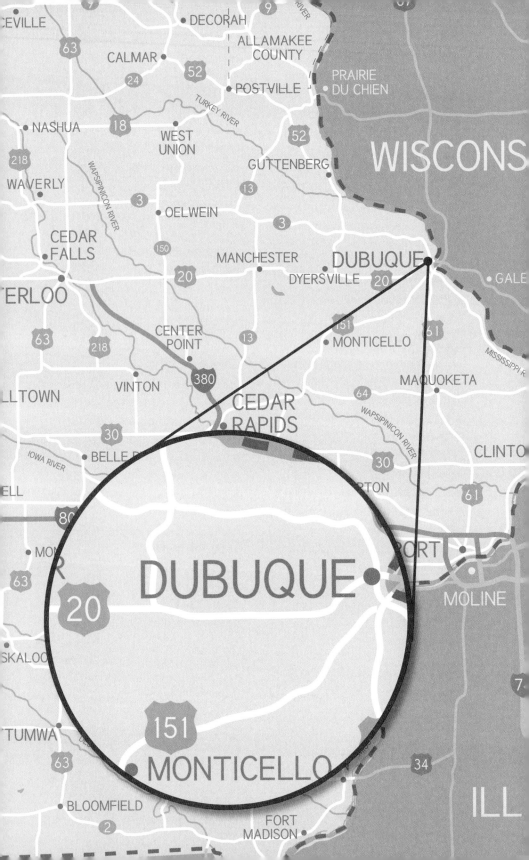

DUBUQUE

DUBUQUE IS WHERE Iowa started and is Iowa's oldest city. Today, it is a bustling town along the Mississippi River where visitors enjoy river life and learn about its history. The National Mississippi River Museum & Aquarium offers an incredible river experience. The local food scene is strong, as many restaurants are proud that they source local food. With Iowa's four distinct seasons, Dubuque offers everyone something year-round. Summer offers warm summer nights hanging out on the Mississippi River. Spring bursts with vibrant green as new life begins to form. Fall offers terrific views of color that can only be found in Dubuque. Winter brings the opportunity to cross-country ski on the many trails nearby. Art enthusiasts will also appreciate the street art throughout the town. A four-season river town is what you will find when you spend a perfect day in Dubuque.

National Mississippi River Museum & Aquarium

350 E 3rd St. • 563-557-9545 • rivermuseum.com

✓ The National Mississippi River Museum & Aquarium sits along the Mississippi River and showcases its history and evolution. Several hands-on experiences are available for kids throughout the museum. The interactive **RiverWorks Splash Zone** on the second floor is for kids of all ages where they can explore rivers. When was the last time you steered a boat downriver through the locks on the Mississippi River? You can view pythons, toads, turtles, owls, bald eagles, and river otters, just to name a few of the animals you may see on your visit. There are several displays throughout that feature the first river people. An authentic dugout canoe made by Native Americans and paddled from Minnesota to Dubuque in the 1860s is on display. Special activities are available for purchase, including stingray feedings. No matter your reason for visiting, you will have a wonderful time visiting this museum in Dubuque.

National Mississippi River Museum & Aquarium (Courtesy of Sara Broers)

Fenelon Place Elevator (Courtesy of Sara Broers)

Fenelon Place Elevator

512 Fenelon Pl. • 563-582-6496 • fenelonplaceelevator.com

✔ The Fenelon Place Elevator, listed on the National Register of Historic Places, is "the world's steepest, shortest scenic railway." The incline is 296 feet long and takes guests to the top of Fenelon Place. The view from above is stunning as you look over Dubuque. Fall brings incredible foliage featuring orange, green, yellow, and red leaves. You can see Iowa, Illinois, and Wisconsin (three states!) from the top of Fenelon Place. The elevator runs daily from April 1 through November 30. When you board the elevator on Fourth and Bluff Streets, you will most likely look for a place to pay. But you don't pay when you board at the bottom; you pay when you exit at the top. Most people will pay for a round trip, but you can pay for a one-way trip and walk down. Have cash on hand since debit and credit cards are not accepted. Early spring and late fall can be chilly in Iowa, so dress in layers and have a winter hat with you as you climb to the top of Fenelon Place.

Pepper Sprout

378 Main St. • 563-556-2167 • peppersprout.com

✓ Pepper Sprout is one of the finest farm-to-table Iowa experiences you will find. Chef Kim Wolff and her staff will treat you like royalty and make sure you enjoy your meal. Your night at Pepper Sprout will be one you talk about for a long time. The menu is seasonal and locally sourced when possible. Small plates include spicy garlic shrimp, a loaded cauliflower bowl, or an andouille sausage corn bread pudding. There's nothing like a homemade andouille corn bread pudding with a crawfish creole sauce in Iowa! If you are a macaroni and cheese lover, you can enjoy the best macaroni and cheese in the state. Pepper Sprout's beef Philly macaroni and cheese is not only unique but a fan favorite. In addition, a traditional beef tenderloin with bacon and red wine shallot butter will never disappoint. And, of course, there are desserts. The Chef's Choice is prepared fresh daily. Make Pepper Sprout your evening destination, and you won't be disappointed.

Pepper Sprout
(Courtesy of Sara Broers)

Nearby Alternatives

Outdoors: Mines of Spain

The Mines of Spain, an outdoor recreation area, is located south of Dubuque. The area is designated a National Historic Landmark and includes the **Julien Dubuque Monument**. Hiking or cross-country skiing are popular activities. As one of Iowa's most "Watchable Wildlife Areas," you may see bald eagles, white-tailed deer, hawks, or even a flying squirrel.

8991 Bellevue Heights Rd. Ste. B
563-556-0620
minesofspain.org

Public Art: Murals of Dubuque

If it's been a while since you have visited Dubuque, you will be surprised. More than 40 murals have popped up in Dubuque since 2016. **Voices Production**, a volunteer, nonprofit organization, is passionate about art and community. Stroll through the downtown area, and you will quickly see why the art scene thrives.

1585 Central Ave.
voicesproductions.org

Restaurant: Brazen Open Kitchen

Brazen Open Kitchen and Bar serves up comfortably stylish New American cuisine featuring locally sourced foods. This destination restaurant serves world-inspired cuisine and cocktails. Chef Kevin Scharpf will make sure you enjoy your freshly prepared meal. Located in the **Millwork District**, this restaurant is one you will be talking about for quite some time.

955 Washington St.
563-587-8899
brazenopenkitchen.com

Museum: Dubuque Museum of Art

The Dubuque Museum of Art, Iowa's first cultural institution, was founded nearly 150 years ago as the Dubuque Art Association. Today, you can view art that spans the 19th century to today. Iowa's Grant Wood is featured, as well as Edward S. Curtis's *The North American Indian*. Traveling exhibits are featured throughout the year, giving you a reason to return for a visit.

701 Locust St.
563-557-1851
dbqart.org

Trip Planning

Travel Dubuque
280 Main St.
800-798-8844
traveldubuque.com

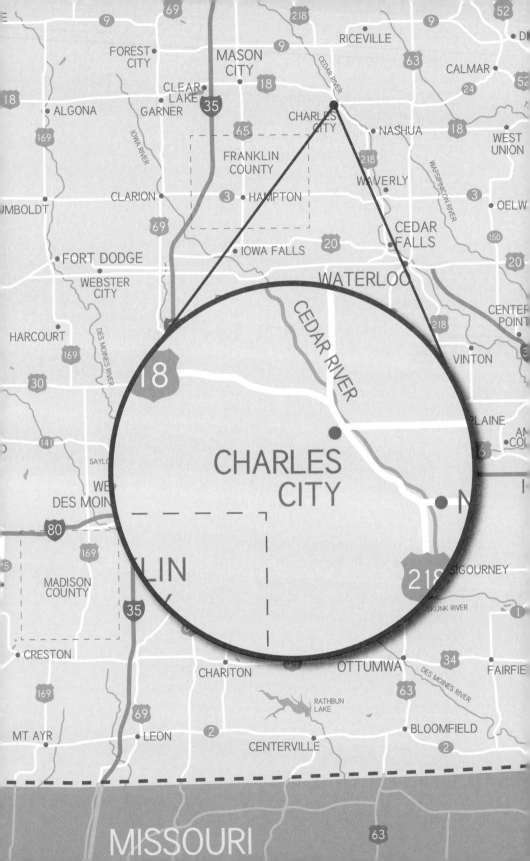

CHARLES CITY

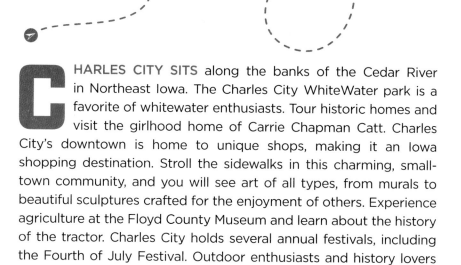

HARLES CITY SITS along the banks of the Cedar River in Northeast Iowa. The Charles City WhiteWater park is a favorite of whitewater enthusiasts. Tour historic homes and visit the girlhood home of Carrie Chapman Catt. Charles City's downtown is home to unique shops, making it an Iowa shopping destination. Stroll the sidewalks in this charming, small-town community, and you will see art of all types, from murals to beautiful sculptures crafted for the enjoyment of others. Experience agriculture at the Floyd County Museum and learn about the history of the tractor. Charles City holds several annual festivals, including the Fourth of July Festival. Outdoor enthusiasts and history lovers will fall in love with Charles City. With fewer than 10,000 residents, this community will win you over in a heartbeat.

The Rustic Corner

413 N Main St. • 641-228-2657 • therusticcorner.com

✓ The Rustic Corner believes your journey begins when you head out the door to visit their business on Main Street. It is the area's most prominent award-winning Hallmark Gold Crown Store. Summer kicks off the holidays with an Ornament Premiere and other events leading up to Christmas. Everything Hallmark can be found here, from greeting cards and keepsake ornaments to unique kids and baby gifts. Create a one-of-a-kind gift at the **Grab It-Engrave It-and Go**. Personalize more than 500 items to give to yourself or gift to someone else. Design your creation with a personalized message, making this the perfect stop for any gift. Handbags, quality toys, sensational scented candles, and books to soothe your soul make the Rustic Corner your next shopping experience in Iowa.

The Rustic Corner (Courtesy of Sara Broers)

The Pub on the Cedar (Courtesy of Sara Broers)

The Pub on the Cedar

101 N Jackson St. • 641-228-3855 • thepubonthecedar.com

✔ Charles City's Pub on the Cedar is where the locals hang out. From pizza to burgers, The Pub on the Cedar serves traditional Iowa favorites as well as a nice selection of salads. The Pub on the Cedar often teams up with local organizations for fundraisers, as the restaurant owners enjoy giving back to others. Grab an outdoor seat to view the Cedar River during the warmer months. Bar seating, as well as table seating, is available in the restaurant. The Pub on the Cedar is also an excellent family gathering venue. For your best experience, call ahead to reserve a table. Your perfect day in Charles City ends with a delightful meal served with love and a whole lot of passion.

Charles City WhiteWater

700 Riverside Dr. · 641-228-4234 · ccwhitewater.com

✓ The Charles City WhiteWater park came to fruition in 2011 and has never looked back. With three distinct features, the course is playable at multiple river flows and skill levels. Kayakers, stand-up paddle boarders, tubers, fishermen, and all river enthusiasts enjoy Charles City WhiteWater. The course is open all year, and it is free to use. Tube and canoe rentals are available by contacting the Charles City Area Chamber of Commerce. **Dam Drop, Doc's Drop**, and **Exit Exam** each have their own challenges on the course. Beginners will adore Dam Drop, and the more experienced whitewater rafters will appreciate Doc's Drop. Exit Exam is the last feature, and it features beginner and intermediate surfing and freestyle moves. If you are curious about what whitewater rafting is all about, go to the entry area at Riverfront Park.

Tip: Multiple access points, including an ADA boat ramp, are located within the park for park-and-play enthusiasts plus upstream and downstream access for float-through adventures.

Charles City WhiteWater (Courtesy of Sara Broers)

Nearby Alternatives

History: Carrie Chapman Catt Girlhood Home

The Carrie Chapman Catt Girlhood Home showcases the life and involvement in the women's suffrage movement of Carrie Chapman Catt. The home is listed on the National Register of Historic Places and is open for tours from Memorial Day to Labor Day.

2379 Timber Ave.
641-228-3336
catt.org

Art Gallery: Mooney Art Collection

The Mooney Art Collection is in the Charles City Public Library and is free to visit. The Mooney collection is an extensive collection of original paintings, engravings, etchings, drypoints, and other art by well-known artists, including Grant Wood. The collections were given to the city in 1941 by famous photographer and Charles City native Arthur Mooney.

106 Milwaukee Mall
641-257-6319
charles-city.lib.ia.us/about/mooney-gallery

Shopping: Prologue Books & Wine

A bookstore with wine, you say? Prologue Books & Wine is where you can read, sip, and repeat. Be inspired by this creative space and enjoy the love of reading. This locally owned bookstore understands the word community, from book clubs to local events.

213 N Main St.
641-220-8567
prologuebooksandwine.com

Trip Planning

Charles City Area Chamber of Commerce Tourism
401 N Main St.
641-228-4234
charlescitychamber.com

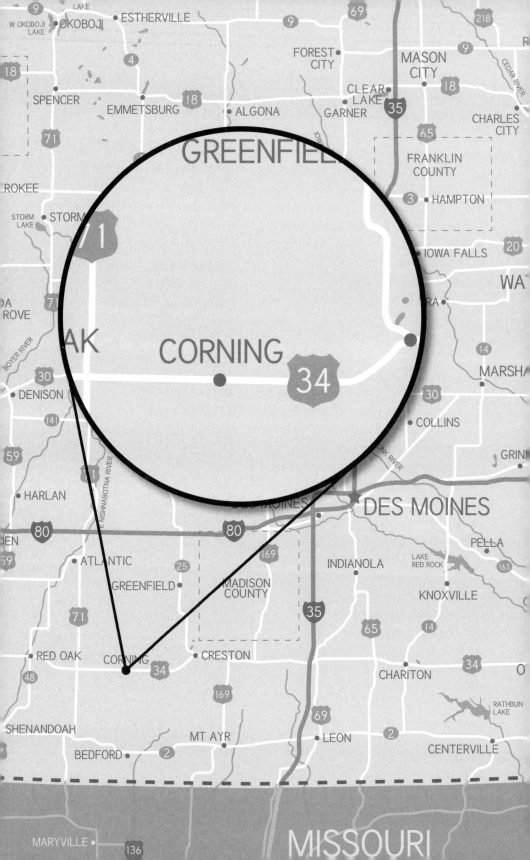

CORNING

CORNING IS ONE of those small towns that jumps out at you as you drive in on Main Street. The beautiful, refurbished Corning Opera House quickly catches your eye as you drive through town. Numerous shows are featured at the historic opera house throughout the year. Historic places are numerous throughout the area, including the French Utopian Icarian Village. Outdoor recreation is strong in the area, with Lake Icaria nearby. Corning is also a part of the area in Iowa that features the Loess Hills, offering incredible views and scenery. Primrose, an award-winning restaurant serves up a winning meal, promises that you will not leave hungry. Fun fact: Corning is the birthplace of entertainment legend Johnny Carson. His childhood home is open for tours, festivals, and other events. With fewer than 2,000 residents, Corning is a small town that knows how to play big.

Primrose

619 Davis Ave. • 641-322-3444 • facebook.com/primrosecorning

☑ Chef Joel Mahr had always wanted to own his own farm-to-table restaurant. How could he say no when an opportunity presented itself in small-town Corning? "City Dining in a Small Town" is the tagline for Primrose, making it a venue you don't want to miss. Chef Joel and his wife, Jill, are the proud owners of this award-winning restaurant. The menu changes seasonally and includes local meat featuring lamb, chicken, and pork. Reservations are suggested so you are not disappointed to arrive and find no seats available. A full bar and a mixologist make this your go-to place for a margarita in Corning. Bring your girlfriends, family, extended family, or significant other for a date night. Primrose in Corning will quickly become your favorite Iowa restaurant.

Primrose (Courtesy of Sara Broers)

Corning Opera House (Courtesy of Sara Broers)

Corning Opera House

800 Davis Ave. • 641-418-8037 • corningoperahouse.com

☑ The Corning Opera House is a treasure that the citizens of Corning restored in the early 2000s. In 1993, the building was placed on the National Register of Historic Places. Around this time, people began to talk about what the opera house could be. The building was empty for several years, and in 2000, a group of dreamers created a restoration committee. Through many bake sales, soup suppers, and grants, the Corning Opera House was ready to be introduced to the community in 2012. Regular events are now held at the opera house. **First Friday Friends** is a popular event. On the first Friday of each month, people gather at the opera house to learn about something new, from farm safety to critters at the lake. Concerts, author talks, and plays are all regular happenings at the Corning Opera House. Plan to visit and enjoy the venue that more than 50,000 people have visited.

Johnny Carson Birthplace

500 13th St. • 641-322-5229 • facebook.com/johnnycarsonbirthplace

☑ Entertainment legend Johnny Carson was born in Corning on October 23, 1925. His birthplace house has been restored to the 1925 era. The small, white house has been well kept, and the signage out front makes it noticeable as you approach the home. You can tour the home and see the room that he was born in. Immerse yourself in the fascinating history of the early life of one of the greatest entertainers ever. Johnny Carson knew how to make people laugh, and he encouraged people to enjoy life. When you tour the home, a video recaps Johnny's life and long career in entertainment. Corning is a good place to start if you have always wanted to know more about Johnny Carson. "Here's Johnny!"

Johnny Carson Birthplace (Courtesy of Sara Broers)

Nearby Alternatives

Museum: French Icarian Village

The French Icarian Village is one of Iowa's best-kept secrets. In Adams County, near Corning, this historical site features the restored refectory, schoolhouse, and cemetery of America's longest-lived, nonreligious utopian society. Schedule a tour and immerse yourself in this interesting way of life.

2349 220th St.
515-321-9743
icaria.net

Outdoors: Lake Icaria

Lake Icaria County Park near Corning offers a campground, six full-service cabins (handicap accessible), eight sleeper cabins, and two cottages. Boating, waterskiing, and fishing are popular outdoor activities in this Iowa county park. Hiking and several picnic areas are also popular in the park.

1756 Juniper Ave.
641-322-4793
mycountyparks.com/county/
adams/park/-lake-icaria.aspx

Coffee Shop: Background's Coffee Bar & Boutique

Walk through a hair salon and then find yourself at Background's Coffee Bar & Boutique. From various handcrafted hot and cold coffee drinks to simple sandwiches, your day will start on the right foot with a quick breakfast or lunch. Kick back and relax on the back porch featuring outdoor seating.

708 Davis Ave.
641-322-5074
facebook.com/
backgroundscoffee

Art: Adams County Freedom Rock

The Freedom Rock for Adams County in Corning is dedicated to three men from Adams County who lost their lives in service. Visit **Memorial Rock Park** to take a moment to reflect on the sacrifices these three soldiers from Adams County made.

406 6th St.
641-322-5229
adamscountyiowa.com/visit/
adams-county-freedom-rock

Trip Planning

**Adams Community/
Corning, Iowa**
710 Davis Ave.
641-322-5229
adamscountyiowa.com

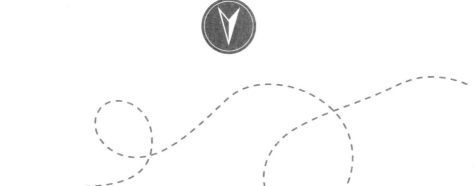

OTTUMWA

OTTUMWA IS WHERE Iowa meets the world. The residents of Ottumwa represent more than 40 countries. This brings a diverse culture, various menus at unique restaurant experiences, and an opportunity to attend incredible events. This Southeast Iowa town thrives on festivals and events. Ottumwa Oktoberfest, the Longest Table, and headliner concerts at Bridge View Center make Ottumwa an event destination. With approximately 600 acres, the 22 parks in Ottumwa are something you can always enjoy. Ride your bike on the trails, enjoy a picnic lunch, or sit in solitude, watching the birds soar across the clear blue skies. Main Street Ottumwa is a thriving organization that continually works to create an inviting downtown. Each day, something new and exciting happens on Main Street. Enjoy lunch at the Canteen and explore Art Alley. If it's been a while since you have spent time in Ottumwa or have never been, give it a chance. You will be glad you visited.

Airpower Museum

22001 Bluegrass Rd. • 641-938-2773 • antiqueairfieldia27.com

☑ There is nothing like standing on a runway home to antique airplanes. The Airpower Museum is a treasure in Ottumwa. The museum is outside of town and offers an incredible aviation museum. Everything and anything related to aviation can be found in the 20,000 square feet available for display. It's not every day that you can stand near a collection of aircraft that are flown regularly. The highlight of the year is when the Antique Airplane Association and the AirPower Museum team up to host an Invitational Fly-In. Several hundred antique airfield pilots fly in over Labor Day weekend, offering visitors a once-in-a-lifetime experience. The passion shown to "Keep the Antiques Flying" is evident as soon as you enter the museum. The Gone West Memorial sits next to the Airpower Museum. People who have passed and were involved in the world of antique airplanes are remembered here. The museum is open year-round, and a donation is suggested for admission.

Airpower Museum (Courtesy of Sara Broers)

Botanitas Isa-Aby's (Courtesy of Sara Broers)

Botanitas Isa-Aby's
1306 W 2nd St. • 641-954-8240 • isa-abys.com

✓ If you are looking for a "hole in the wall" restaurant with incredible food, look no further than Botanitas Isa-Aby's. You can not only shop for Mexican foods but also enjoy a fresh Mexican meal. This restaurant is a family affair; daughter Aby will often greet you. She handles the orders, and other family members manage the grill and the kitchen. The parking lot is small, but don't let that sway you from dining in. The tasty recipes that Sandra, the owner, creates will leave your mouth watering for hours. She and her family travel annually to Mexico to bring back recipes that are current there. The slushy is the most popular item, made up of refreshing fresh fruit juices frozen and served in a cup featuring fresh pineapple, coconut, papaya, and mango flavorings. The menu is not extensive; it's right on point with tacos, tortas, quesadillas, and rice the top menu items. Order them with your preferred meat, and you will have a winning meal. Daily specials offer something new, so don't be afraid to ask.

American Gothic House Center

300 American Gothic St., Eldon • 641-652-3352
americangothichouse.org

The American Gothic House Center is in Eldon, a small rural Iowa community. Ottumwa is 16 miles from Eldon, a short drive to the scene of one of America's most famous paintings. In 1930, Grant Wood took a tour of Eldon and spotted a little white house with a large Gothic window. He quickly sketched the house while in Eldon and returned home to Cedar Rapids to paint his most recognized piece, *American Gothic*. The visitor center welcomes travelers from near and far. An exhibit gallery featuring the life and times of Grant Wood is inside the center with a gift shop. You can also grab a pitchfork, an apron, and bib overalls in the visitor center. You can then walk 40 feet and pose in front of the American Gothic House. The grounds are open from dusk to dawn, meaning you can view the house during daylight hours. The parking lot is large enough for an RV, and the visitor center is handicap accessible.

American Gothic House (Courtesy of Sara Broers)

Nearby Alternatives

Outdoors: Pioneer Ridge Nature Area

Pioneer Ridge Nature Area offers hiking, camping, mountain biking, cross-country skiing, and horseback riding experiences. Sleep in a cabin or camp on one of the campsites. Fishing is popular in the four stocked ponds. Wildlife viewing and an indoor nature center make this a fun family experience.
1339 US Hwy. 63, Bloomfield
641-682-3091
wapellocounty.org/conservation/ parks/pioneer_ridge_nature_area

Restaurant: Top Hat Coffee and Entertainment

There are many coffee shops in Ottumwa. Top Hat Coffee and Entertainment answers the call for an upscale coffee experience in the **Main Street Ottumwa District**. The specialty drinks and quirky decor make this a fun place to kick off your day.
228 E Main St.
641-814-9129
facebook.com/tophatottumwa

Shopping: Sassy Sunflower Boutique

The Sassy Sunflower Boutique features sunflowers, trendy clothing, and Iowa-branded products. Sassy Sunflower is the place to go if you are looking for a new outfit to make your day. It's located next door to the **Sassy Java House**, so pick up a cup of coffee after you shop.
2465 Northgate St.
641-682-8731
sassy-sunflower.square.site

Entertainment: Bridge View Center

The Bridge View Center offers top headliner concerts throughout the year. The entertainment is topnotch, so you don't have to travel to a big city to pay for parking and extreme hotel prices. Take advantage of the walking trail outside of the Bridge View Center and take in the beauty of the Des Moines River.
102 Church St.
641-684-7000
bridgeviewcenter.com

Trip Planning

Meet Ottumwa
102 Church St.
641-684-4303
meetottumwa.org

DAVENPORT

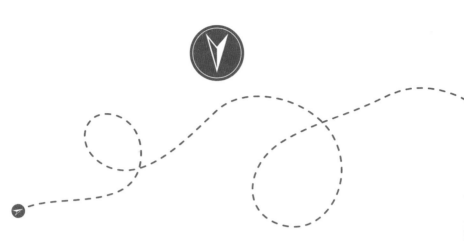

DAVENPORT, ONE-FOURTH OF the Quad Cities, is a city on the Mississippi River in Eastern Iowa. In Davenport, you can see works of art at the Figge Art Museum that date back to the 15th century and even those closer to the present. The downtown area is bursting with festivals and events all year long, including the Festival of Trees, Mississippi Valley Blues Festival, and the Quad-City Times Bix 7. The Historic Village of East Davenport offers six square blocks of shopping and entertainment. If you want to go on a home tour, drive through McClellan Heights and admire the various architectural styles. For a quiet experience, visit one of several parks, including the Vander Veer Botanical Park and Conservatory. If you are looking for a lot of energy, the busy, energetic nightlife scene is alive and well in Davenport. The year-round activities will make your day perfect and make it easy to start planning your return trip.

Vander Veer Botanical Park and Conservatory

215 W Central Park Ave. • 563-326-7818 • davenportiowa.com/government/
departments/parks_recreation/locations/vander_veer_botanical_park

✓ The Vander Veer Botanical Park and Conservatory is believed to be one of the first botanical parks west of the Mississippi River. The conservatory is famous for its 100-year tradition of providing gardens under glass. Spring brings azaleas, summer brings tropical foliage, fall includes the **Chrysanthemum Festival**, and winter features the **Poinsettia Lights Display**. Many older trees make up the gardens, with some dating back to the early 1890s. Christmas offers festive magic at Vander Veer. The holiday lights and Christmas plants will get you into the holiday spirit. **The Enabling Garden** is accessible and features plantings that stimulate the senses, including planting beds and containers raised for comfortable reach. Physical barriers are limited, making this garden accessible for all. The Vander Veer Botanical Park and Conservatory will brighten your day no matter what time of year you visit. There is no admission fee, and the park is open all year.

Vander Veer Botanical Park and Conservatory
(Courtesy of Sara Broers)

Figge Art Museum (Courtesy of Sara Broers)

Figge Art Museum

225 W 2nd St. • 563-326-7804 • figgeartmuseum.org

✔ At the Figge Art Museum, you can choose your own museum adventure. Several exhibitions come and go, but many stay. The beauty of exhibitions coming and going is that they give you an excellent reason to return for a visit. The permanent collection is extensive, and the pieces are circulated regularly. The museum's comprehensive collection of Grant Wood pieces includes Wood-designed furniture. One of the first collections of Haitian art in the United States is on display in the museum. Several programs and events are held throughout the year, which is a great way to introduce artists, international and local projects, and films to the public. There's always something going on at the beautiful Figge Art Museum. Your general admission ticket does include admission to any special exhibitions. On-site parking is free. If the lot is full, there is free street parking nearby. The Second Street entrance is wheelchair accessible. Wheelchairs are also free on a first-come, first-served basis at the museum. Plan to spend at least two hours at the Figge Art Museum, as you will find something new around every corner.

Lagomarcino's

2132 E 11th St. • 563-324-6137 • lagomarcinos.com

☑ Lagomarcino's has been serving up the finest chocolates since 1908. Boxed chocolates, custom orders, and an old-fashioned soda fountain will greet you as soon as you walk through the doors. The unique chocolates are fun to admire. When did you last see a chocolate baseball that looked like a real one? Lagomarcino's does everything well. This fourth-generation family-owned business continues to evolve and bring the quality everyone has grown to love and expect. On my first visit, I quickly learned that this family-owned business has a story of success. If you dine in for lunch, expect a potato salad just like grandma used to make and a sandwich that is the perfect accompaniment. Dessert is calling; of course, it's a hot fudge sundae. Lagomarcino's friendly staff will welcome you like family during your visit to Davenport. You will quickly become knowledgeable about the business, and make sure you walk out with a box of chocolates.

Lagomarcino's (Courtesy of Sara Broers)

Nearby Alternatives

Museum: Putnam Museum and Science Center

The Putnam Museum and Science Center is a history and natural science museum. With more than 250,000 artifacts, the exhibits are continually changing. The science center offers a hands-on experience, making it a family-friendly museum. You can easily spend three hours exploring the Putnam Museum and Science Center.
1717 W 12th St.
563-324-1933
putnam.org

Restaurant: Mo Brady's Steakhouse

Dine on an Iowa steak at Mo Brady's Steakhouse. Iowa Premium Beef is sourced from local family farms. Pair your perfectly cooked steak with a potato, side salad, and bread pudding for dessert. You'll understand why, according to Mo Brady's Steakhouse, the best beef comes from Iowa.
4830 N Brady St.
563-445-0684
mobradyssteakhouse.com

Outdoors: Centennial Park

Davenport's Centennial Park is a 250-acre urban public park that straddles the Mississippi River. Fishing spots, basketball courts, a skateboard park, and several gazebos make this the perfect park to relax in at the end of every day. I enjoy finding a bench and watching the birds on the Mississippi River.
315 S Marquette St.
563-326-7711
davenportiowa.com/government/
departments/parks_recreation/
locations/centennial_park

Entertainment: Rhythm City Casino Resort

Rhythm City Casino Resort offers gambling, a spa, and entertainment in this Davenport event center. Several on-site restaurants offer buffets, a steak house, and a market. To enjoy the thrill and the excitement of a casino, roll the dice and give the Rhythm City Casino and Resort a try.
7077 Elmore Ave.
563-328-8000
rhythmcitycasino.com

Trip Planning

Visit Quad Cities

1601 River Dr., Ste. 110
Moline, IL
800-747-7800
visitquadcities.com

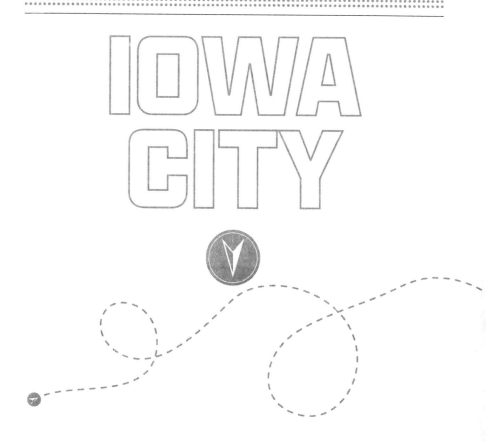

IOWA CITY

OWA CITY IS home to the University of Iowa, where the Iowa Hawkeyes hail from. Coralville and North Liberty are two incredible communities that encompass the Iowa city metro area. Iowa City is home to Old Stone Capitol, the building that served as the seat of state government for 16 years. Today, you can tour this National Historic Landmark, currently used by the University of Iowa. The Old Capitol Museum is free to visit and open to the public. Downtown Iowa City has fun shopping and excellent mom-and-pop restaurants with home-cooked food. The Iowa River Landing Sculpture Walk features sculptures that are created by an Iowa artist and is based on a work in the Iowa Writer's Library. The town bleeds gold and black, so becoming an Iowa Hawkeye for the day is easy. Serious mountain bikers will appreciate Sugar Bottom Recreation Area. It has single-track trails that surround Lake Macbride. The time you spend in Iowa City will only make you crave more.

University of Iowa Athletics Hall of Fame

2425 Prairie Meadow Dr. • 319-384-1031
hof.hawkeyesports.com

✓ The University of Iowa Athletics Hall of Fame is every Iowa Hawkeye's dream. Three floors of Hawkeye memories are housed in this venue. It is free to visit, and you will be inspired to become a Hawkeye fan after your visit. If you have never attended an Iowa Hawkeye event, you will find yourself hurrying to find tickets to the next event. If you are already an avid Hawkeye fan, you will quickly recognize the players' names in the University of Iowa Athletics Hall of Fame. Trophies from the National Championship and Orange Bowl, along with Nile Kinnick's Heisman Trophy are on display. The interactive room is open to Hall of Fame guests touring the facility and event attendees. The museum exhibits continue to grow as the Iowa Hawkeyes win awards. Visit to enjoy the feeling of being an Iowa Hawkeye.

University of Iowa Athletics Hall of Fame
(Courtesy of Sara Broers)

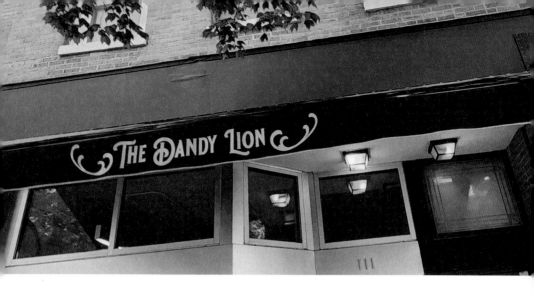

The Dandy Lion (Courtesy of Sara Broers)

The Dandy Lion

111 S Dubuque St. • 319-358-6400 • thedandylionic.com

✔ The Dandy Lion is a dandy little luncheonette in Downtown Iowa City. "Kitchen, coffee, and cocktails" is its tagline. Breakfast at the Dandy Lion is the perfect way to kick off your day in Iowa City. The Standard consists of two perfectly cooked eggs served your way. Add-ins include bacon, ham, sausage, or veggies, with hash browns and your favorite toast. You could also substitute Impossible sausage for meat or eggs for no extra charge. You can get your breakfast the way you want it. It's not uncommon to see University of Iowa students dining in this local diner. The food is good, and the servers are spot-on regarding customer service. Omelets, pancakes, and a house-baked cinnamon roll round out a fantastic breakfast menu. The Dandy Burger is a lunchtime favorite, consisting of two thin beef patties, a brioche bun, cheddar cheese, and chowchow sauce. It's a roaring good meal. Want something lighter? Grab soup or salad. This eclectic restaurant will make you a fan in one meal.

Antique Car Museum of Iowa

200 E 9th St., Coralville • 319-569-4504
antiquecarmuseumofiowa.org

The Antique Car Museum of Iowa is home to more than 80 automobiles dating from 1899 to 1965. The history of transportation, as well as antique cars, is showcased in this museum. If you are a fan of antique license plates, this museum has a collection of antique Iowa license plates on display. What I love about this museum is that the cars come and go. Private collections are shared for a period, and then another collection moves in. It's not uncommon to see a 1954 Chevy, a Willys Knight, or a 1924 Ford Model T. If you don't think you enjoy antique cars, try this museum. Every car has a story, and if you think about it, your personal vehicle also has a story. If you are looking for a unique venue for your next event, the Antique Car Museum of Iowa may be what you are looking for. With more than 25,000 square feet and a "few" beautiful automobiles, there's a good chance that you will have the most talked about event in your circle of friends. You can easily spend a good two hours in this museum.

Antique Car Museum of Iowa (Courtesy of Sara Broers)

Nearby Alternatives

Roadside Attraction: World's Largest Wooden Nickel

The World's Largest Wooden Nickel measures 16 feet in diameter and has been standing in Iowa City since 2006. It is located near a busy road. There is no specified parking area, but pulling off and viewing this fun roadside attraction is easy.

3246 Iowa River Corridor Trail
roadsideamerica.com/tip/18697

Restaurant: Vue Rooftop

The Vue Rooftop sits on the 12th floor of the Hilton Garden Inn Iowa City. Enjoy a craft cocktail, bar bites, steak, scallops, and a view of Iowa City that you will not find elsewhere. Popular outdoor seating is first come, first served. Kick back and relax in contemporary seating with the best rooftop view in Iowa.

328 S Clinton St.
319-519-4650
vuerooftop-ic.com

Shopping: The Shop Iowa City

Vintage finds, along with handcrafted art, apparel, and accessories, are what you will find at the Shop Iowa City. Three friends gathered together and created the Shop Iowa City. Vintage finds, along with handcrafted art, apparel, and accessories are waiting for you. Step into the Shop Iowa City for "modern vintage" and thoughtfully curated items.

4 S Dubuque St.
319-519-6305
theshopiowacity.com

Walking Tour: Literary Tour

The Iowa Writers' Workshop at the University of Iowa has made Iowa City rich in literacy. Take a walking literary tour starting with the Dey House, home of the Writers'. Established in 1936 as the first creative writing degree program in the United States, the Iowa Writers' Workshop alumni include 17 Pulitzer Prize winners, six recent US Poets Laureate, and numerous winners of the National Book Award and MacArthur Foundation Fellowships.

507 N Clinton St.
319-337-6592
thinkiowacity.com/things-to-do/
arts-culture/literary-tour

Trip Planning

Think Iowa City

900 1st Ave. Hayden Fry Way, Coralville
319-337-6592
thinkiowacity.com

CEDAR RAPIDS

CEDAR RAPIDS IS in the heart of Eastern Iowa and is a cultural hub. From theater to live music, there's always a theatrical or musical production to attend. Minor league baseball holds the hot ticket yearly during baseball season for a Cedar Rapids Kernels game. History comes to life through Grant Wood and the area's passion for the Czech community. Fresh local food is featured in numerous restaurants throughout Cedar Rapids, making it a destination for foodie experiences. Outdoor adventures continue all year long. From cross-country skiing in the winter to biking the more than 49 trails, an outdoor adventure awaits you. The craft brewery scene continues to grow as the breweries work to create destination experiences. Your soul will be enriched with art as you experience more than 30 murals throughout the downtown area of Cedar Rapids. You can easily spend an entire day, weekend, or a week in Cedar Rapids. The parks are bursting with color when August rolls around, but don't let this keep you from visiting other times of the year. Each park offers something unique, such as boating, historic homes, or golf. However you decide to spend your time in Cedar Rapids, you won't be disappointed. My guess is that you will be planning your return visit before you depart.

Cedar Rapids Museum of Art

410 3rd Ave. SE • 319-366-7503
crma.org

☑ With more than 7,800 works of art, the Cedar Rapids Museum of Art will inspire you. The world's largest collection of works by Iowa's beloved Grant Wood can be found here. As with many art museums, the permanent collection is phenomenal. The permanent exhibits change throughout the year, giving you a reason to plan a return visit. Special docent-guided tours can be arranged throughout the year during regular museum hours. Contact the museum to schedule your visit if you want an in-depth tour. The Cedar Rapids Museum of Art owns and operates the **Grant Wood Studio**. It's important to note that the studio, or the facilities are not handicap accessible. Other art is showcased, including an incredible display of Roman art. In 1996, Cedar Rapids art collectors Tom and Nan Riley generously donated 21 significant Roman portrait busts to the museum. From permanent collections to exhibitions, the Cedar Rapids Museum of Art will leave you with a new appreciation of art.

Cedar Rapids Museum of Art (Courtesy of Sara Broers)

Brucemore (Courtesy of Sara Broers)

Brucemore

2160 Linden Dr. SE • 319-362-7375 • brucemore.org

The beautiful Brucemore estate reflects over 140 years of history throughout the complex. The mansion, outbuildings, gardens, landscape, and collections will provide you with a "wow factor." The Brucemore grounds are open daily with seasonal hours to explore independently. On your visit, utilize the **History Ungated Digital Landscape Tour**. Scan the QR codes with your smartphone at various points of interest to learn more about the estate. Contact the Brucemore staff for specific information on tours of the mansion, programs, or a special themed tour of the stunning landscape. Pets are welcome on the outdoor grounds but must be leashed. Events are held throughout the year and offer something unique for each season. Arts, music, **Nooks and Crannies Tours**, and the popular **Holiday Tours** are some of the special events you can participate in. No matter what time of year you visit, Brucemore will quickly make you want to return.

Tip: May offers incredible colors throughout the gardens.

Zeppelins Bar & Grill

5300 Edgewood Rd. NE • 319-393-3047 • zeppelinscr.com

✔ Cedar Rapids's food scene is filled with deliciousness. Zeppelins Bar & Grill is known for its quality and top-notch service. And don't forget the drinks- including draft beer, wine, the popular Moscow, Razzleberry, or Cucumber Mule. The Zeppelin Burger is always a safe bet. A half-pound Angus beef patty, applewood-smoked bacon, cheddar cheese, barbecue sauce, and crispy onion tanglers on a brioche bun for the win! Are you hungry now? A plant-based burger patty is also offered on the menu. A full rack of smoked barbecue ribs is always an excellent choice. House-smoked pork ribs with a traditional barbecue or raspberry barbecue sauce are served with brown sugar-bacon baked beans and buttermilk chive mashed potatoes. The Mediterranean chicken salad is always refreshing if you are looking for a lighter meal. Enjoy your meal and hang out at the bar; you will always find "Iowa nice" at Zeppelins Bar & Grill.

Zeppelins Bar & Grill (Courtesy of Sara Broers)

Nearby Alternatives

Outdoors: Indian Creek Nature Center

The Indian Creek Nature Center has been open for 50 years and offers incredible outdoor and indoor spaces. A highlight of any visit is the 200 acres that offers more than five miles of hiking through restored wetlands, prairies, and woodlands.

5300 Otis Rd. SE

319-362-0664

indiancreeknaturecenter.org

Shopping: NewBo City Market

The NewBo City Market is a unique space dedicated to health, happiness, and well-being. Local talent is showcased through entrepreneurship. Grab lunch at one of the businesses and purchase products from farmers and artisans. NewBo City Market also hosts guest vendors throughout the year at pop-up shops and Saturday farmers and artisans markets.

1100 3rd St. SE

319-200-4050

newbocitymarket.org

Museum: National Czech & Slovak Museum & Library

The National Czech & Slovak Museum & Library offers lifelong learning in the community through cultural connections. Freedom, identity, family, and community live through generations sharing their traditions and stories. Numerous exhibits come and go throughout the year, showcasing the universal themes of culture, freedom, democracy, and immigration. Art classes and events are also offered throughout the year.

1400 Inspiration Pl. SW

319-362-8500

ncsml.org

Restaurant: Tomaso's Pizza

A local favorite in Cedar Rapids is Tomaso's Pizza. Chicago deep dish, Detroit deep dish, and New York thin crust are served up at Tomaso's. Add the toppings of your choice, from pepperoni to sauerkraut; unique specialty pizzas round out the menu. Voted "Best Pizza In Town" 12 times! **Tip:** ask for the local beers on tap.

2706 1st Ave. SE

319-364-4313

tomasos4me.com

Trip Planning

Cedar Rapids Tourism

370 1st Ave. NE

319-731-4560

tourismcedarrapids.com

AMANA COLONIES

THE AMANA COLONIES is a short 30-minute drive from Cedar Rapids and the Iowa City area in east-central Iowa. Today, there are seven villages on 26,000 acres: Amana, East Amana, High Amana, Middle Amana, South Amana, West Amana, and Homestead. This German communal community lived here until 1932. Now, you can experience what life was like during that time when you visit this National Historic Landmark. Shopping attracts thousands of yearly visitors, as several mom-and-pop entrepreneurs produce locally made products. Antiques enthusiasts will appreciate the antiquing scene throughout the Amana Colonies. Furniture, woolen blankets, scarves, quilts, brooms, and homemade chocolate fudge are just some things you can expect to find in the Amana Colonies. No matter when you visit, you can be sure to find Christmas. The International Christmas Market in the Amana General Store is a must-experience when in Amana.

International Christmas Market

4423 220th Trl., Amana • 319-622-3692 • amanacolonies.com/places/
united-states/iowa/amana/gifts-books/international-christmas-market

✓ The International Christmas Market is in the General Store in Amana. This year-round Christmas wonderland is sure to bring a smile to your face. The scent of pine will remind you that Christmas can be experienced during any time of the year. As you stroll through the market, the extensive array of Christmas trees will inspire you to change up your family's Christmas tree. The festive shopping environment features unique gift ideas and traditional Christmas decor for you and your family to enjoy. You can visit 365 days a year for an incredible Christmas experience. Get a head start on your Christmas shopping in your shorts and T-shirt the summer. There's nothing like listening to Christmas carols and shopping for Christmas decorations in the Amana Colonies in July.

International Christmas Market (Courtesy of Sara Broers)

Schanz Furniture and Refinishing (Courtesy of Sara Broers)

Schanz Furniture and Refinishing

2773 Hwy. 6 Trl., South Amana
319-622-3529 · schanzfurniture.com

In 1966, Norman and Joanna Schanz opened Schanz Furniture in the Amana Colonies. In 1996, Norman's son Mike became one of the craftsmen and now carries on the family tradition of furniture making. Each of the craftspeople has over 20 years of experience. You can expect a quality product when you shop at Schanz Furniture and Refinishing. Each piece of furniture is hand-built with select solid hardwood. If you need a different style of woodwork, the team can assist you. Their creativity will shine through your request. In this woodshop, it's all about you and your furniture. There are no cookie-cutter pieces, as each piece is extraordinary. You will see the signature of the person who crafts your furniture, approving the quality of their work. A lot of furniture from here becomes a family heirloom, making memories with one piece of wood at a time.

Millstream Brau Haus

741 47th Ave., Amana • 319-622-7332 • millstreambrauhaus.com

✓ The Millstream Brau Haus in Amana is a German-style pub with locally brewed beers from **Millstream Brewing Co.** You can expect a "one of a kind" experience when you dine at the authentic German *bierhalle*. The German-themed menu has items listed in both English and German. Drunken Schnitzel Fingers (*Betrunkene Schnitzelfinger*) is a breaded pork schnitzel cut into strips covered in their homie sauce and topped with bacon. I don't know about you, but anytime I see the word bacon, sign me up! The dessert menu offers a bountiful selection, including bread pudding. The flavor of bread pudding changes with the season, and it is some of the best I have had in Iowa. The drink menu features Saturday Night Pants, Back Road Stout, and Farmer's Tan from Millstream Brewing Co. Hard apple ciders are also on tap, along with fine Amana wines. No matter what you are in the mood for, the atmosphere and experience will win you over at Millstream Brau Haus.

Tip: Order the bread pudding!

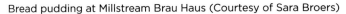

Bread pudding at Millstream Brau Haus (Courtesy of Sara Broers)

Nearby Alternatives

Outdoors: Kolonieweg Trail
The Kolonieweg, or **Colony Way**, is a five-mile trail connecting the villages of Amana and Middle Amana. Scenic views of Lily Lake, the Millrace, pastures, farmland, and the beautiful countryside dot this trail. Hop on your bicycle and explore the Amana Colonies by bicycle; you will be glad you did.
iowabytrail.com/find-a-trail/122/kolonieweg-trail

Unique Lodging: Hotel Millwright
Hotel Millwright offers lodging in a historic mill complex. This up-to-date hotel sits next to Iowa's only remaining textile mill. The blankets and linens are all made at the **Amana Woolen Mill**. Stay and play in Amana at Hotel Millwright, as Amana is all within walking distance of your hotel room.
800 48th Ave., Amana
319-838-5015
hotelmillwright.com

Restaurant: Ox Yoke Inn
Visitors to Amana have been dining at the Ox Yoke Inn since 1940. Your group will enjoy a meal served family style at this classic family restaurant. Top-notch hospitality and a hearty homestyle meal featuring German and American favorites will fill your belly.
4420 220th Trl., Amana
319-622-3441
oxyokeinn.com

Shopping: Amana General Store
The Amana General Store is a must-stop for everyone visiting the Amana Colonies. Home and kitchen supplies, along with snacks for the whole family, can be purchased at the Amana General Store. Handcrafted gifts featuring Amana-made products will fill your shopping bag to the brim.
4423 220th Trl., Amana
319-622-7650
amanashops.com

Trip Planning

Amana Colonies Convention & Visitors Bureau
622 46th Ave., Amana
319-622-7622
amanacolonies.com

IOWA FALLS

"IOWA FALLS, THE Scenic City," is in North Iowa. The Iowa River flows through a beautiful limestone gorge, making it one of Iowa's most scenic towns. And, of course, Iowa Falls has gorgeous waterfalls known as the "rapids of Iowa." The charming Main Street is bursting with several locally owned shops. A recent renovation has taken this Main Street to a new level of awesomeness. From bookstores to specialty women's clothing shops, there is something for everyone on Iowa Falls's Historic Main Street. You can indulge in barbecue and fine dining at Red's Smokehouse. New to Iowa Falls is a speakeasy on the upper floor of Red's. If you catch Iowa's oldest popcorn stand open—STOP! A variety of flavors are available at this iconic stop in Iowa Falls. When was the last time you crossed a swinging bridge? You can do that in Iowa Falls.

Scenic City *Empress* Riverboat

1113 Union St. • 641-648-9517
empressboatclub.org

The Scenic City *Empress* Riverboat is part of the Scenic City *Empress* Boat Club. The club was formed during the Great Depression, as it was an opportunity for families to gather and enjoy special times together. Fast-forward several years, and today it is a central hub for community events. Public cruises are offered on the weekends and provide a great view of the Iowa River. The clubhouse lodge has recently undergone renovations. An updated dock, firepit, canoe access, and the lodge exterior have been restored. This beautiful area in Iowa Falls is a great place to picnic before boarding the riverboat. The Scenic City *Empress* Riverboat is the last operating riverboat on the inland water in Iowa for viewing natural and scenic river heritage. Board the 50-passenger double-decker pontoon boat for a memorable day in Iowa Falls.

Scenic City Empress Riverboat (Courtesy of Sara Broers)

Red's Smokehouse (Courtesy of Sara Broers)

Red's Smokehouse

410 Washington Ave. • 641-500-3119 • redssmokehouse.com

Red's Smokehouse offers barbecue, baby back ribs, salmon, salads, and steak. What a find! Make sure to come hungry for that tasty meal you have been longing for. Distinctive lunch and dinner specials are must-tries at Red's Smokehouse. Red's also delivers a delicious shrimp salad. Looking for a new twist on macaroni and cheese? How about a barbecue Mac Bowl?! The presentation of any plate at Red's Smokehouse is mind-blowing. Time, love, and flavors all go into each dish served. Dessert choices vary from carrot cake to white chocolate cobbler cheesecake. The upper floor offers a unique experience: a speakeasy. Plan to dine, drink, and enjoy the ambiance at this destination restaurant in Iowa Falls.

Calkins Nature Area

18335 135th St. • 641-648-9878 • hardincountyia.gov/calkins-nature-area

☑ Calkins Nature Area boasts 76 acres of rolling hills nestled along the banks of the Iowa River. An amphitheater hosts programs and different events throughout the year. You can explore the park with three miles of hiking trails. A highlight for many who visit is the butterfly house, which features native wildflowers and butterfly species. A full-size Plains Native American tepee is also on-site. For those who enjoy birding, the Calkins Area Nature Center is hopping with birds all season long. After exploring outdoors, stop indoors at the **Native American and Natural History Museum**. The museum is home to one of Central Iowa's largest collections of Native American artifacts. Admission is free to the public. Lace up your hiking boots and enjoy exploring the Calkins Nature Area.

Calkins Nature Area
(Courtesy of Sara Broers)

Nearby Alternatives

Outdoors: Iowa Falls Swinging Bridge

Walk across the Iowa Falls Swinging Bridge by accessing the bridge through **Assembly Park** or **Rocksylvania Road**. View the beautiful limestone that towers along the Iowa River and enjoy crossing one of Iowa's great swinging bridges. Cross any time of year, but fall is the most colorful view of the river.

Rocksylvania Rd.
641-648-5549
iowafallschamber.com

Art Collection: Pat Clark Art Collection

The Pat Clark Art Collection was given to the Ellsworth College Foundation in 1997. Pat Clark, a native of Iowa Falls, wanted residents of her hometown to have a "window on the international world of art." Admission is free, and guided tours are offered by appointment.

520 Rocksylvania Ave.
641-648-8576
patclarkart.org

Shopping: Ugly Peanut Boutique

The Ugly Peanut Boutique offers personal styling and free local delivery. This fun boutique carries current clothing styles to help you look your best. Jewelry and other accessories are also available to round out your new look. There's no need to leave small-town Iowa for big-city shopping; Iowa Falls has it at the Ugly Peanut Boutique.

523 Washington Ave.
641-872-9629
uglypeanutboutique.com

Restaurant: Princess Grill & Pizzeria

The Princess Grill & Pizzeria, in operation for more than a century, is famous for its pizza, ice cream, and soda fountain. Located on the Iowa Falls's historic Main Street, the restaurant fits right in with its retro appearance. Don't miss the rotating lunch specials, including soups, salads, pastas, and sandwiches in addition to their extensive menu.

607 Washington Ave.
417-648-9602
facebook.com/profile.php?id=100063831421353

Trip Planning

Iowa Falls Chamber of Commerce/Main Street
520 Rocksylvania Ave.
641-648-5549
iowafallschamber.com

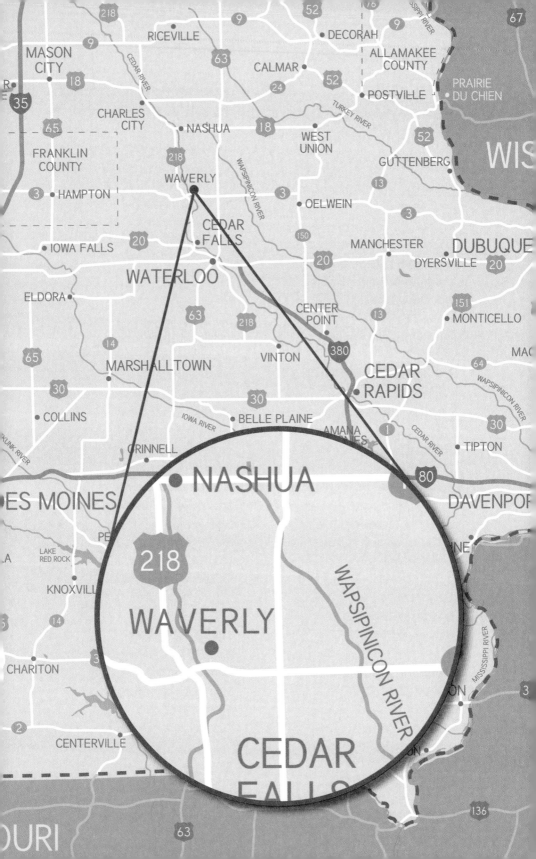

WAVERLY

WAVERLY IS A small college town northeast of the Waterloo and Cedar Falls metro areas. It is located on the banks of the Cedar River and is home to 10,000 residents. Waverly's downtown district is designated as an "Iowa Main Street." Outdoor activities are numerous, with several city parks, a soccer complex, and a rail trail. In winter, the parks are popular for cross-country skiers and snowshoers. Bird enthusiasts love the Waverly area, as birding is strong in the many wooded areas. If you are looking for a small-town feel, Waverly has that and more. The community embraces all four seasons, with festivals all year long. Several mom-and-pop restaurants are ready to welcome you, including Wild Carrot. Bring the family and enjoy the great outdoors in Waverly. Wartburg College is known for its music program. Do not be surprised to find a concert happening somewhere in town since music is loved and respected in Waverly.

The Mixing Bowl

214 E Bremer Ave. • 319-830-3562 • facebook.com/mixingbowlwaverly

☑ The Mixing Bowl is a well-loved bakery on Waverly's Main Street. The cake pops, cookies, pies, and breakfast rolls are hot items. Once you step into the Mixing Bowl, the aroma of baked goods will take you away. Whole pies are available for purchase, and it's suggested that you order ahead. Donuts by the dozen and fried cinnamon rolls are also available for order. The best tip I can give you is to visit early in the day. The shelves will be stocked with fresh baked goods. As the day goes on, the shelves clear out rather quickly. You can pick up an order or kick back and enjoy a view of Waverly's Main Street as you indulge in the goodies from this fantastic bakery. There's nothing like fresh baked goods served up with a smile. It's a guarantee that you will be back for more!

The Mixing Bowl (Courtesy of Sara Broers)

Cedar Bend County Park (Courtesy of Sara Broers)

Cedar Bend County Park

1267 250th St. • 319-882-4742
mycountyparks.com/county/bremer/park/cedar-bend-park.aspx

✓ Cedar Bend County Park is the largest park in Bremer County and is on the outskirts of Waverly. The park sits on the edge of the Cedar River, making it a dream park for outdoor enthusiasts. A wide variety of outdoor recreational opportunities include kayaking, hiking, and birding. This is an all-season park, as cross-country skiers enjoy the trails during the winter months. The gates close to the park in the winter, but you can walk in. A well-shaded campground features more than 60 campsites with electrical hookups on a first-come, first-served basis, and flush toilets and showers are also available. This park is a winner with three sand volleyball courts, three horseshoe pits, and a specified canoe launch area. The large trees offer shade and incredible views while hiking in the park.

Bremer County Historical Society

402 W Bremer Ave. • 319-352-1862
bremercountyhistoricalsociety.org

☑ Waverly's Bremer County Historical Society has set hours from May through October. Volunteers run the museum and share their passion for the area with all visitors. Highlights of the museum are a log cabin, schoolroom, Bremer County history, and a Veteran's Room. The museum's first floor is a tribute to the Bremer County men and women who have served their country as part of the armed forces. The Rohlf Bedroom is a highlight of the museum. Dr. W. A. Rohlf helped establish St. Joseph Mercy Hospital in Waverly. It was one of the premier medical facilities in Northeast Iowa. The bedroom suite showcases the craftsmanship of an earlier time. The Rohlf family owned and used all furnishings in the room for many years. Guided group tours are available; contact the museum to schedule your visit.

Bremer County Historical Society (Courtesy of Sara Broers)

Nearby Alternatives

Restaurant: The Wild Carrot

The Wild Carrot is known for its sandwiches, soups, salads, and desserts. Breakfast and lunch are served with a taste of deliciousness. Are you looking for a unique gift or two? The Wild Carrot has special gift items, as well. Hand-painted greeting cards, Iowa-themed mugs, and a variety of jams and jellies make delightful gifts to remember your perfect day in Waverly.

215 E Bremer Ave.
319-352-2215
facebook.com/wildcarrotwaverly

Outdoors: Prairie Links Golf Club

Prairie Links Golf Club offers an 18-hole golf course and an event center. With spacious watered fairways and large elevated greens, this course is excellent for the beginner or experienced golfer. Grab a sandwich or drink after your round at the **Prairie Patio and Grill**.

19 Eagle Ridge Dr.
319-242-7675
prairielinksgolf.com

Shopping: Root

Root launched in October 2013 and has grown to be a well-respected business in the Midwest. Krista Dolash, owner and founder, wants you to experience nontoxic hair-care, skin-care, and cleaning products. A stop in this shop can lead you to a healthier lifestyle.

100 E Bremer Ave.
319-290-5746
rootpretty.com

Entertainment: Wartburg Community Symphony

The Wartburg Community Symphony showcases the talent of Wartburg students and Waverly natives. From jazz to fairy-tale operas, there's a show for everyone. All concerts are held in **Neumann Auditorium** on the **Wartburg Campus**. The music program is a highlight for the community.

100 Wartburg Blvd.
319-352-8370
www.wartburg.edu/symphony

Trip Planning

Waverly Chamber of Commerce

118 E Bremer Ave.
319-352-4526
waverlyia.com/
chamber-of-commerce

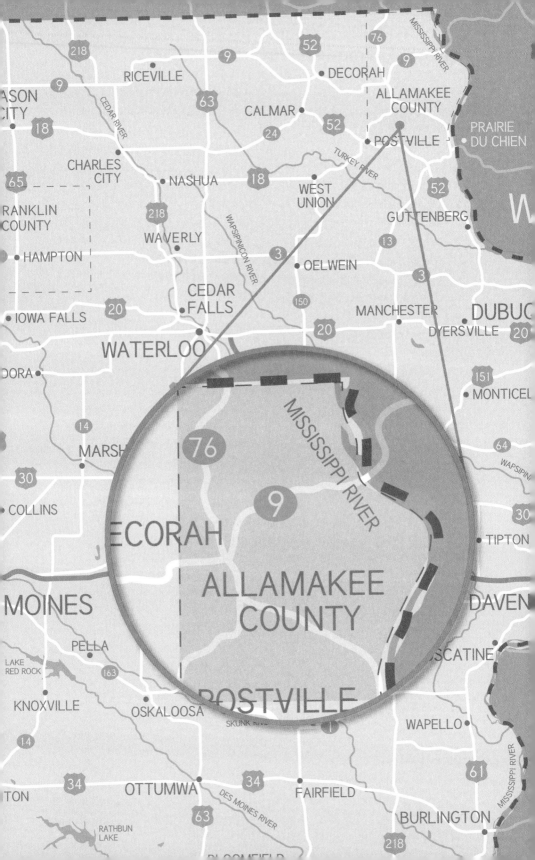

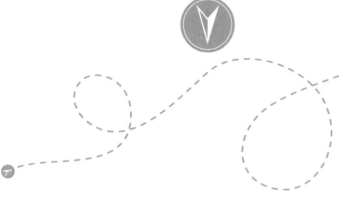

ALLAMAKEE COUNTY

ALLAMAKEE COUNTY IS in the Driftless Area of Iowa in Northeast Iowa. The bluffs, rugged valleys, cliffs, and incredible views throughout the county are some of the best in the country. The Yellow River Water Trail is one of Iowa's most remote and scenic rivers. River enthusiasts will enjoy kayaking, canoeing, fishing, and scenic experiences. Hikers will appreciate the more than 50 miles of hiking trails in Yellow River State Forest. Lansing connects the Driftless Area Scenic Byway and the Great River Road National Scenic Byway. Waukon, known as "the Cheese Curd Capital of Iowa," is home to WW Homestead Dairy and some of the best dairy products in the country. The beautiful Driftless Area Education and Visitor Center in Lansing is a fantastic place to learn about life on the Mississippi River and in Allamakee County. Fall is my favorite time of year to visit, as the fall foliage is some of the best in the nation.

Effigy Mounds National Monument

151 Hwy. 76, Harpers Ferry
563-873-3491 • nps.gov/efmo/index.htm

✓ Effigy Mounds National Monument, in Harpers Ferry, is a sacred space in Iowa. With more than 200 American Indian mounds, it is a special place in the Upper Mississippi River Valley. This site is open year-round, and it is free to visit. The visitor center hours vary by season, with closures on major holidays. Cellular service may be spotty, so don't depend on this being a high-connectivity area. Effigy Mounds National Monument is the perfect place to disconnect and reconnect with nature. The visitor center, museum, auditorium, park store, and one-mile round-trip boardwalk are accessible to wheelchairs. Marching Bear Hike features the largest effigy mound group in the monument, featuring 10 bear-shaped and three bird-shaped effigy mounds. There are no driving tours in the park; a hike will be involved if you want to see the mounds. I would encourage you to visit during all four seasons, as the views and ambiance change with the seasons.

Effigy Mounds National Monument
(Courtesy of Sara Broers)

Lid's Bar and Grill (Courtesy of Sara Broers)

Lid's Bar and Grill

1350 9th St. SW, Waukon • 563-568-2388
facebook.com/profile.php?id=100063669248863

✔ Lid's Bar and Grill in Waukon offers a supper club atmosphere and a private party room. Fresh hand-packed burgers are a local favorite, along with the daily specials. How about hamburger gravy over mashed potatoes, corn, and a roll? Sounds like a meal that Grandma used to cook. Save room for dessert, as the pie lady bakes pies to enjoy. You can indulge in an award-winning tenderloin, as Lid's Bar and Grill won Iowa's 2022 Best Pork Tenderloin. Top your tenderloin with mayo, lettuce, and a toasted bun, and you have a winning sandwich. The appetizers are always a hot item: fried pickles, fried green beans, onion rings, and portabella mushrooms, to name a few. This local establishment continues changing its menu while continually offering the best home-cooked meals in Allamakee County.

Driftless Area Education and Visitor Center

1944 Columbus Rd. · 563-538-0400
allamakeecountyconservation.org/driftless-center

✓ The newly constructed Driftless Area Education and Visitor Center is nestled beneath limestone bluffs with incredibly scenic views of the Mississippi River. I love that this education center showcases why the Driftless Area exists and how people used to live there. There is a rich tradition of Native Americans in the area, along with European and American settlements in Northeast Iowa. This area of Iowa has a large population of bald eagles, and during the winter months, they are incredibly beautiful to view along the Mississippi River. Several hands-on activities are offered for youngsters, making it a great stop for families with younger kids. I have always felt that this center is the perfect size, just right for all visitors, young and old, to visit. The Driftless Area Education and Visitor Center is free to visit.

Driftless Area Education and Visitor Center (Courtesy of Sara Broers)

Nearby Alternatives

Shopping: Horsfall's Variety Store

Horsfall's Variety Store in Lansing is a destination store. This family-owned business will wow you as you stroll the aisles. Spend at least two hours sifting through your finds; you will find something, from cosmetics to bulk spices to greeting cards to candy-making supplies to duct tape to puzzles to lawn decor. It's been said, "If you can't find it at Horsfall's, you don't need it."
300 Main St., Lansing
563-538-4966
facebook.com/hfvariety

Outdoors: Yellow River State Forest

The Yellow River State Forest offers more than 8,900 acres of an outdoor paradise. Camping, hiking, mountain biking, fishing, hunting, and equestrian riding are all popular activities. Hike any trail with binoculars in tow; you will surely experience incredible views.
YRSF, 729 State Forest Rd.
Harpers Ferry
563-586-2254
iowadnr.gov/places-to-go/state-forests/yellow-river-state-forest

Restaurant: Skinny Dip
The Skinny Dip is a local favorite in Lansing. It is home to the best ice cream in Northeast Iowa. Burgers, shakes, hot dogs, chili dogs, and malts are highlights of the menu. This seasonal stop is a must when you are in Allamakee County.
115 N 2nd St., Lansing
563-217-0878
facebook.com/lansingskinnydip

Museum: Allamakee County Historical Museum & Genealogy Research Center

Waukon's Allamakee County Historical Museum & Genealogy Research Center is housed in the beautiful original courthouse built in 1861. For tours, call ahead to arrange a visit. The museum operates seasonally but will open by appointment. Attractions include an 1874 one-room schoolhouse and an 1870 log cabin full of period artifacts.
121 Allamakee St. NW, Waukon
563-568-2954
allamakeehistory.org/museum

Trip Planning

Visit Allamakee County
101 W Main St., Waukon
563-568-2624
allamakeecounty.com

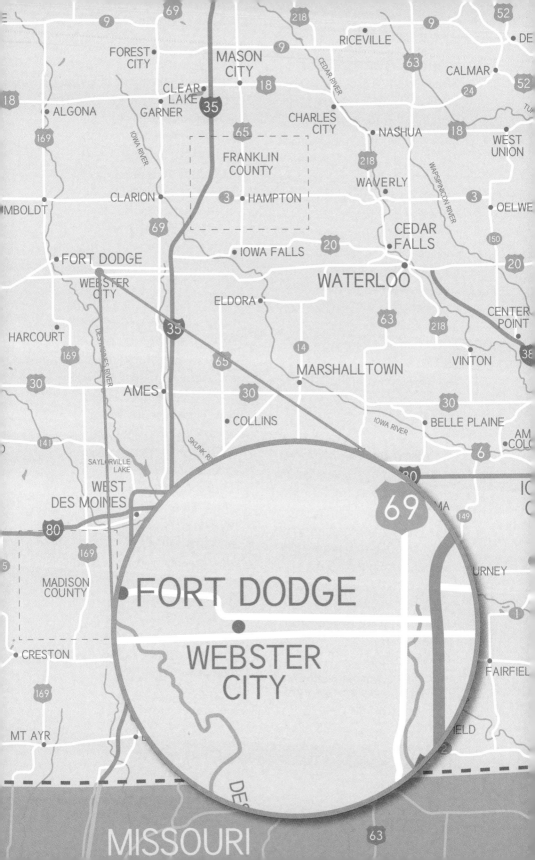

WEBSTER CITY

WEBSTER CITY OFFERS small-town charm in the northern part of Iowa. Outdoor adventures, and a walkable downtown, make this Iowa community appealing to many. The Webster Theater was recently renovated and is a treasure the community appreciates today. Entrepreneurship is strong in Webster City, and it shows on Main Street. Leon's Pizza is a favorite stop of mine when I am in town. From the pizza to broasted chicken, Leon's will serve a hot, tasty meal every single time. If a pork tenderloin is calling your name, you need to visit the Grid Iron Grill & Sports Bar. Conquer the Iowa Tenderloin Trail and pair your tenderloin with homemade onion rings. Drive on part of the longest stretch of highway in the United States through Webster City. Webster City sits on Historic Route 20, the longest stretch of highway in the United States, stretching 3,365 miles from Massachusetts to Oregon. No matter how you choose to spend your time in Webster City, you will quickly learn that the people of the community appreciate your visit.

The Webster Theater

610 2nd St. • 515-832-6684 • webstertheater.org

☑ Rain or shine, a movie theater is always a great place to spend time. The Webster Theater was set to close after a large factory in Webster City closed its doors, leaving hundreds unemployed. The community realized that the local theater was an important place to gather. In 2013, a significant undertaking took place. Volunteers worked hard to reopen the doors to the theater through a lot of blood, sweat, and tears. The fundraising paid off, and today, families enjoy movies together at the Webster Theater. Webster City is an excellent example of how people can pull together to save historic buildings. Main Street is bustling, partly due to the Webster Theater being open. Communities all across the country can appreciate what has happened in Webster City.

The Webster Theater (Courtesy of Sara Boers)

Briggs Woods Park and Golf Course (Courtesy of Sara Boers)

Briggs Woods Park and Golf Course

2490 Briggs Woods Trl. • 515-832-9570 • mycountyparks.com/county/hamilton/park/briggs-woods-park-and-golf-course.aspx

✓ Briggs Woods offers an 18-hole golf course along with 82 camping sites. At Briggs Woods, you can tent camp or pull into one of the level pull-through sites with a large motorhome. Wi-Fi is available in the campground. Beautiful cabins are available for rent all year long. Pets are not allowed in the cabins or shelters at the park. Several styles of cabins are available, as one cabin will accommodate 15 people. During the warmer months, you can rent bicycles, kayaks, and canoes at Briggs Woods Park. Shuttle service is not provided, but the rental company will take your kayaks and canoes to the lake. I enjoy riding my bike on the 5.7-mile paved walking trail that connects Briggs Woods to Webster City. The round trip of 11 miles makes for a nice bike ride. Canoeing, fishing, and swimming are also popular on the 70-acre lake.

Tip: Pack a picnic lunch to enjoy on the trail.

Leon's Pizza

643 2nd St. • 515-832-2215 • facebook.com/profile.php?id=100063482592671

✓ Leon's Pizza has been serving delicious food on Main Street for over 50 years. Locals enjoy broasted chicken, burgers, garlic bread with cheese, and, of course, pizza. Specialty pizzas such as an all-vegetable, Hawaiian, or chicken bacon ranch offer something a little different from the traditional all-meat pizza. If chili is your thing, Leon's serves up a nice, warm bowl of chili. The folks at Leon's will welcome you anytime. If there's one thing for certain, you will feel like part of the Leon's Pizza family once you dine there. Dine in or grab your meal to go and enjoy it in one of several city parks. It's not uncommon for people to travel many miles to dine for a meal here. A recent Facebook post stated, "Wish I was 86 miles closer, best chicken and pizza." Grab it while you can—Leon's Pizza will be worth every bite.

Leon's Pizza (Courtesy of Sara Boers)

Nearby Alternatives

Historic House: The Jane Young House

The Jane Young House is a historic home that sits next door to the beautiful Kendall Young Library in Webster City. The Webster City Women's Club has met in the home for 100 years. Today, you can tour the historic home and view the lovely interior.

629 Elm St.
515-297-0846
janeyounghouse.com

Restaurant: Grid Iron Grill & Sports Bar

The Grid Iron Grill & Sports Bar is proud to be on Iowa's Tenderloin Trail. Indulge in an award-winning Iowa pork tenderloin or enjoy a rib eye, grilled chicken breast, Grid Iron Classic, or hot beef! Enjoy the aptly named and creative "Warm-ups" and football-themed classics while working through a bucket of beers during a game.

1121 E 2nd St.
515-832-2255
gridirongrillia.com

Outdoors: Arts R Alive

At Arts R Alive in West Twin Park, new sculptures are installed each May, making this someplace you will want to keep coming back to see. Beautiful, stunning sculptures offer beauty to the park and an opportunity for you to appreciate art. This is free for everyone.

1100 Superior St.
artsralive.org

Shopping: Heart N Home Interiors and Gifts

Heart N Home Interiors and Gifts offers specialty shopping, including jewelry, florals, candles, cards, home decor, women's clothing, and other fun items. This shop is more than a place; it's where you will feel at home. Creating fresh looks and lasting impressions is their mission for customers. Seasonal home decorations are perfect take-home reminders of your perfect day in Webster City.

1423 Superior St.
515-832-1457
heartnhomeia.com

Trip Planning

Webster City Area Chamber of Commerce

628 2nd St.
515-832-2564
visitwebstercityiowa.com

OKOBOJI

THE OKOBOJI AREA of Iowa is known as the Iowa Great Lakes. Everyone loves the lakes that make up the Okoboji area. This incredible chain of lakes extends several miles from the Minnesota border southwest and covers approximately 15,000 acres. Iowa's largest natural lake, Spirit Lake, has five interconnected lakes: West Okoboji, East Okoboji, Upper Gar, Lower Gar, and Minnewashta. West Lake Okoboji is the hub of the chain of lakes and is the gateway to Okoboji's playground, which many adore. Beachgoers will appreciate the beaches in the area. Ride the Legend Roller Coaster at Arnolds Park, the world's 13th-oldest wooden roller coaster. Bring your extended family on your visit to Okoboji, as this area in Iowa is home to many family reunions, year after year. The park is free to visit; only riders need passes to ride the attractions. The Arnolds Park Museum is also home to one of the finest beaches in Okoboji. Take a ride on the *Queen II* for a unique view of the area by water. Enjoy all that Okoboji and the area have to offer.

Arnolds Park Amusement Park

37 Lake St. • 712-332-2183
arnoldspark.com

Arnolds Park opened its doors to the public more than 125 years ago. Most attractions are seasonal, open from Memorial Day to Labor Day. The park is home to the Arnolds Park Museum, the Iowa Great Lakes Maritime Museum, and a wedding venue. It is one of the longest-operating amusement parks in the world. There are several amusement park rides, including a Ferris wheel, a wooden roller coaster, and a log flume water ride. This family-friendly amusement park will quickly win you over. The park is unique, because it is a full-fledged amusement park, yet offers a river cruise and go-karts. It is free for all to visit. Tickets must be purchased for the amusement park rides and some experiences. Visit often, as you are guaranteed to discover something new on each visit.

Arnolds Park Amusement Park (Courtesy of Sara Broers)

Okoboji Store (Courtesy of Sara Broers)

Okoboji Store
1404 Hwy. 71 S · 712-332-5628 · theokobojistore.com

The Okoboji Store is a classic stop for many who visit the area. Its history runs deep. The Original Okoboji Store was built as a skating rink. In 1884, it was converted into a general store, post office, boat rental, and livery. Fast-forward to the late 1980s, a boat store was added to the property, making the Okoboji Store a destination. Many travel specifically to dine at the Okoboji Store, so why not make it your go-to restaurant in Okoboji? Order the walleye cakes for a little taste of lake life. Everyone needs to try the walleye when they are in the Iowa Great Lakes Region. Oh, and save room for the county fair mini donuts. The cinnamon-sugar-dusted donuts served with dipping glazes and sprinkles are amazing. No matter what you feel like, the Okoboji Store has you covered. By land or by lake, visit the Okoboji Store using any transportation! Boat valet parking is a unique experience here. Enjoy the views of the lake from the large outside patio or rock out to live music all summer.

Iowa Rock 'n Roll Music Association Hall of Fame & Museum

243 Broadway St. • 712-330-0889
iowarocknroll.com

✓ Iowa's rock and roll history runs deep in the Iowa Rock 'n Roll Music Association Hall of Fame & Museum. Bands, musicians, radio personalities, or anyone who loves music will appreciate all that this museum has to offer. Rock and roll music began in the late 1940s and early '50s. Out of rock and roll, the evolution of blues, jazz, gospel, and country music came to fruition. When you stroll through the museum, reflect on the impact the musicians had on the music industry. You will be touched in some way, shape, or form. Many musicians, including Buddy Holly, have made an impact on Iowa and music over the years. Today, the music lives through the passion that the Okoboji area has for continuing Iowa's rich music traditions.

Iowa Rock 'n Roll Music Association Hall of Fame & Museum
(Courtesy of Sara Broers)

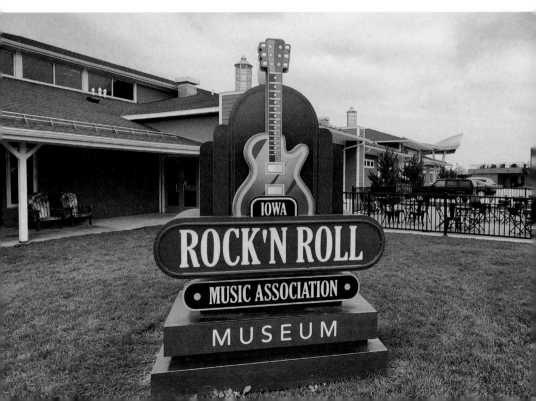

Nearby Alternatives
Museum: Okoboji Classic Cars

The Okoboji Classic Cars museum, in West Okoboji, is a destination for all gearheads. After all, it is nicknamed the "Midwest's Ultimate Man Cave." Take a walk down memory lane with your family and reflect upon the evolution of the automobile.

810 Jeppeson Rd.
West Okoboji
712-332-8029
okobojicc.com

Restaurant: The Waterfront

I'm all about dining with a view in the open air. The Waterfront is a restaurant on the shores of Lake Okoboji. Steak, seafood, pasta, pizza, burgers, and anything your heart desires is on the menu. Kick back and enjoy lake life at its finest.

Tip: Save room for a rustic apple tart. This savory apple dessert is served up with sea salt caramel ice cream.

610 Linden Dr., Arnolds Park
712-220-3200
waterfrontokoboji.com

Entertainment: Superior 71 Drive-In Theater

A short drive 11 miles northeast of Okoboji takes you to one of the last remaining drive-in Iowa theaters. Camp out in the bed of your truck and grab popcorn from the concession stand. See two movies for the price of one under the Iowa dark skies for a priceless experience.

1482 300th Ave., Spirit Lake
712-336-0700
superior71drivein.com

Outdoors: Gull Point State Park

Gull Point State Park is an outdoor enthusiast's dream come true. A 1.5-mile self-guided interpretive trail is a great space for viewing wildlife. Access to fishing and boating is easy at Gull Point State Park. Plan to camp under the stars for an outdoor adventure to remember.

1500 Harpen St., Milford
712-337-3211
iowadnr.gov/places-to-go/state-parks/iowa-state-parks/iowa-great-lakes#gull-point-state-park-76

Trip Planning
Okoboji Chamber of Commerce

565 US Hwy. 71, #4
712-332-2107
okobojichamber.com

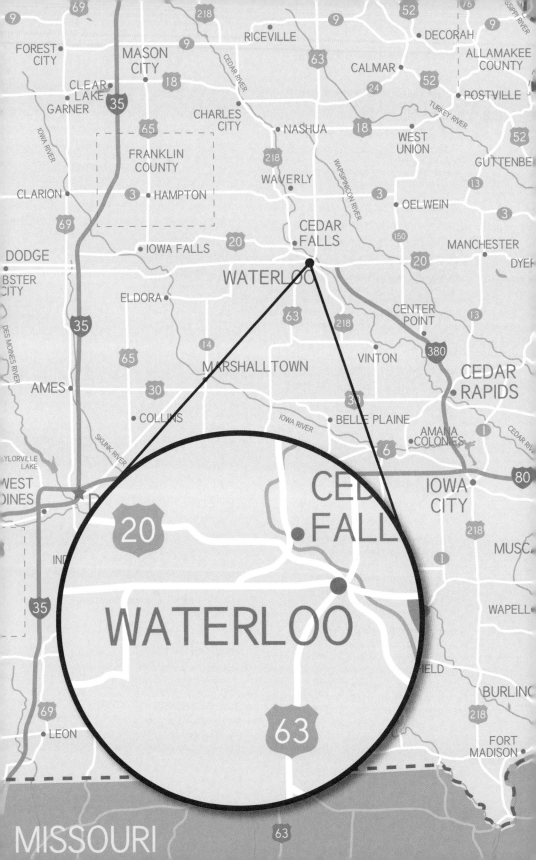

WATERLOO

WATERLOO IS A metro area on the eastern side of Iowa. It is connected with Cedar Falls, a college town that connects with Waterloo. All four seasons come to life in Waterloo through events, trails, and theme parks. March brings the award-winning Irish Festival to town. Summer offers an experience at one of the top 10 waterparks in the United States. You cannot visit Waterloo without learning about John Deere tractors. Visit the John Deere Engine & Tractor Museum to become a tractor expert quickly. The town continues to renovate and repurpose buildings. Locals knew the building as Wonder Bread from previous years. Today, it is home to the popular brewpub SingleSpeed Brewing Company. Outdoor activities include hiking, biking, kayaking, and beautiful gardens. There is no shortage of things to see and do in the area. Enjoy your perfect day in Waterloo!

Lost Island Theme Park

2225 E Shaulis Rd. • 319-455-6700 • thelostisland.com

☑ Lost Island Theme Park offers thrilling attractions with world-class fun for families of all ages. Experience the creation of a tropical oasis in the Midwest. The park areas feature fire, water, spirit, air, and Earth. Volkanu: Quest for the Gold Idol is a 4D interactive adventure ride featured in Mura, meaning fire. The Akua Maze featured in Awa, representing water, is the ideal place for everyone to cool off while dodging a water maze. Are you traveling with toddlers? Star Fish Cove and Tahiti Vilate are perfect for little kids. No matter how adventurous you choose to spend your day, your family will have a fantastic day at Lost Island Theme Park. Visit its sister park, the award-winning **Lost Island Water Park**, less than one mile down the road.

Lost Island Theme Park (Courtesy of Sara Broers)

Cedar Valley Arboretum & Botanical Gardens (Courtesy of Sara Broers)

Cedar Valley Arboretum & Botanical Gardens

1927 E Orange Rd. • 319-226-4966 • cedarvalleyarboretum.org

☑ You can relax and surround yourself in peace at the Cedar Valley Arboretum & Botanical Gardens. Explore the Iowa Native Prairie as the blooms change all season long. I love that this attraction is home to an orchard. Apples, pears, plums, and cherries are all grown here. Find a bench and observe the colorfulness of each tree. Herb gardens are popular, as they showcase how anyone can quickly become a gardener in any size of a space. **The Max and Helen Guernsey Children's Garden** offers programs throughout the year. It features a koi pond, Greenroof playhouse, a hobbit hole, a dinosaur dig, and many other things kids enjoy. There is a small fee to visit. Through generous donations of donors, new buildings and updates are continually being added to this incredible arboretum and botanical garden.

Newton's Paradise Café

128 E 4th St. • 319-234-0280 • newtonscafe.com

☑ If you are looking for something new with a twist, Newton's Paradise Café in downtown Waterloo is to the rescue. Order a traditional breakfast meal featuring pancakes, Iowa French toast (a little powdered sugar and maple syrup drizzle), or biscuits and gravy. And after breakfast, why not return for lunch? This local favorite diner is sure to please your taste buds all day long. Fresh produce and local ingredients are sourced all year long when possible. You can be assured you are supporting locals when you dine at this downtown favorite. Belly up to the diner-style counter or choose a traditional table. I enjoy grabbing an outdoor table when the weather permits. The menu changes now and then, giving you a reason to return for a new food experience. For a traditional Iowa flare, order the Iowa breaded tenderloin. But I'm warning you: the meat will overpower the bun. Enjoy!

Newton's Paradise Café (Courtesy of Sara Broers)

Nearby Alternatives

Museum: John Deere Tractor & Engine Museum

Learn about the history of John Deere at the John Deere Tractor & Engine Museum. This free interactive museum is family friendly. Several hands-on experiences are peppered throughout the museum. John Deere plows, lawn mowers, tractors, and machines are displayed throughout the museum.

500 Westfield Ave.
319-292-6126
visitjohndeere.com

Restaurant: Hibachi Sushi Buffet

Experience a little Japanese culture in Waterloo at the Hibachi Sushi Buffet. Some of the menu choices include egg drop soup, broccoli in hot garlic sauce, shrimp with vegetables, and beef lo mein. Come hungry and enjoy the buffet, a flaming onion tower on the hibachi, or explore classic and innovative sushi rolls.

1535 Flammang Dr.
319-232-6868
hibachisushibuffets.com

Outdoors: George Wyth State Park

George Wyth State Park is often called an "urban sanctuary." This outdoor lover's paradise is in the Cedar Valley, offering fishing, biking, camping, hiking, and birding. With more than three miles of paved trails in the park, you are connected to the popular **Cedar Valley Trail** system.

3659 Wyth Rd.
319-232-5505
iowadnr.gov/places-to-go/
state-parks/iowa-state-parks/
george-wyth-state-park

Sporting Event: Waterloo Black Hawks

The Waterloo Black Hawks, an award-winning men's hockey team in the Cedar Valley, offers exciting events throughout the year. Go and experience the venue or a hockey game. You will quickly learn what all the excitement and energy are about when the puck drops.

125 Commercial St.
319-232-3444
waterloo-black-hawks.square.site

Trip Planning

Experience Waterloo
716 Commercial St.
319-233-8350
experiencewaterloo.com

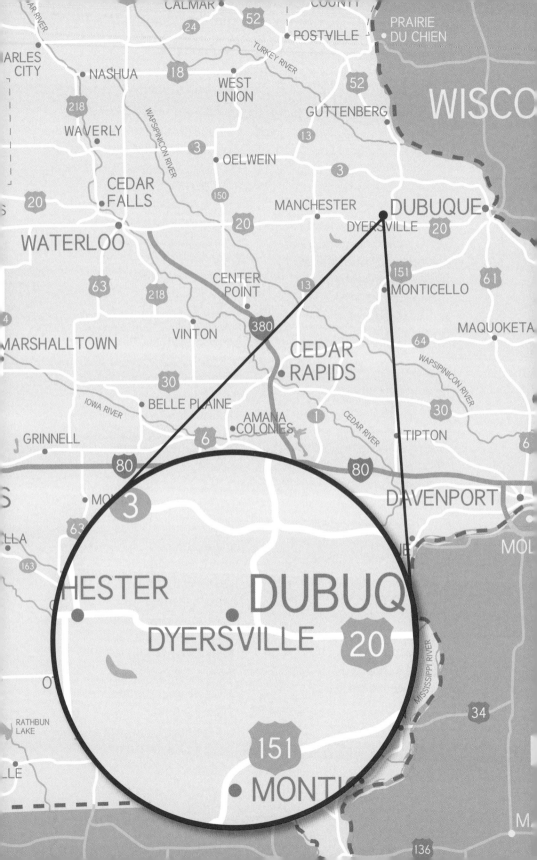

DYERSVILLE

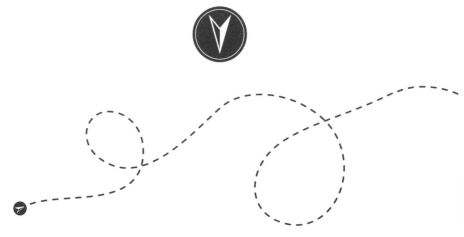

DYERSVILLE IS WHERE many come to keep the game of baseball alive. The *Field of Dreams* Movie Site is inspiring and allows you to walk on the field. If you don't think baseball will interest you, Dyersville is where you need to give it a try. The passion for the game is shown throughout the town. The new If You Build It Exhibit explains how the movie *Field of Dreams* placed Dyersville on the map. With a population of less than 5,000, Dyersville knows how to play big in small-town America. Farm history and toys are on display at the National Farm Toy Museum. Plan to spend a good two hours exploring and learning all about farm toys. A favorite place of mine is the St. Francis Xavier Basilica; it is incredibly beautiful! No matter how you spend your time in Dyersville, this small town will leave you wanting more. Rain or shine, this little Iowa town will make you say, "Wow."

Field of Dreams Movie Site

28995 Lansing Rd. • 563-875-8404 • fieldofdreamsmoviesite.com

The *Field of Dreams* Movie Site will lead you to ask, "Is this heaven? No, it's Iowa." You can stand on the original "Field of Dreams" from the 1989 blockbuster movie of the same name. It's been said that the movie site is more than baseball. This magical baseball field has all the feelings that you would expect to find on an Iowa farm. The field is open from sunrise to sunset all year long. Iowa corn is typically planted in April, and the cornfield near the movie site is harvested the first weekend in November. Home tours are available of the Kinsella family household. You can also spend the night in the newly remodeled three-bedroom farmhouse and enjoy the "Kinsella Experience." The home accommodates up to seven guests. Grab one of the best seats at the ballpark and strike up a baseball game on your visit. Parking is on gravel and grass, and it is free to visit the baseball field. You will have a memory of a lifetime when you visit the *Field of Dreams* Movie Site.

Tip: Bring your baseball glove and a baseball to the site.

Field of Dreams Movie Site (Courtesy of Sara Broers)

St. Francis Xavier Basilica (Courtesy of Sara Broers)

St. Francis Xavier Basilica

104 3rd St. SW • 568-875-7325 • spiresoffaith.com/st-francis-xavier-basilica

The St. Francis Xavier Basilica is one of two basilicas in Iowa. It is one of 53 basilicas in the United States. This incredible structure stands over 76 feet tall. Admire the beauty of each of the 64 burnt-colored cathedral windows in the church. Upon entering the church, you will notice the details that make this place unique. You will be mesmerized by the architectural designs and the decor in the ceilings. The red brick spires tower over this quaint Iowa town, making it visible for miles. Twelve hundred people can sit in the basilica. You can enter the basilica throughout the day or arrange a guided tour. The north and south doors are open from 7 a.m. until 7 p.m. There is a suggested donation of $5 per person who visits. Rain or shine, you can see this attraction in any weather all year. If you are lucky, you may visit during one of the several church services offered throughout the week.

Chad's Pizza

108 1st Ave. W • 563-875-2483 • chadspizza.com/chads-pizza-dyersville

Chad's Pizza is where the locals love to dine in Dyersville. This is a local franchise, making it an Iowa favorite. It is locally owned and has operated for 19 years and counting. The buffet filled with pizza, a salad bar, potato rounds, and broasted chicken is a winner every time. The Friday night buffet offers hand-battered cod, broasted chicken, baked potatoes, pizza, soup, and a salad bar. The menu items will continually keep your taste buds hopping. Gluten-free cauliflower crusts are also an option. It has been voted the Best of the Iowa Pizza Fest and World Champion at the **World Food & Music Festival**. There's a good reason that this is where locals dine and why people travel from miles around to enjoy the pizza. Local wines are also in the house, giving you a real Iowa experience. Bringing the kids? The Kids' Dugout features kids meals with macaroni and cheese, pizza, chicken nuggets, or a kids buffet. No one in your group will leave hungry.

Chad's Pizza (Courtesy of Sara Broers)

Nearby Alternatives

Restaurant: Ritz Restaurant

The Ritz Restaurant, a supper club experience, awaits you in Dyersville. Sit at the bar and enjoy the signature Southern Comfort Old-Fashioned. Popular options include steaks, homemade soups, burgers, and a codfish sandwich. If you are looking for a night out with your significant other, the Ritz is the answer!

232 1st Ave. E
563-875-2268
ritzdyersville.com

Exhibit: If You Build It Exhibit

Learn how the making of America's slice of heaven came to be at the If You Build It Exhibit in Dyersville about the movie *Field of Dreams*. Relive your favorite movie scenes and discover stories from behind the scenes. Learn how the locals helped make baseball magic out of an Iowa cornfield. The small entrance fee is worth every penny.

310 2nd St. SE
563-230-7180
ifyoubuilditexhibit.com

Shopping: Savvy Salvage

Savvy Salvage is a vintage store filled with antiques and oddities. You can also shop for Dyersville memorabilia. It's true; your trash is someone else's treasure. Owner Heidi Huisman established her business in 2010 and has not looked back.

240 1st Ave. E
563-543-8035
savvysalvageiowa.com

Museum: National Farm Toy Museum

The National Farm Toy Museum features more than 70 years of farm toys. In 1945, an out-of-work journeyman molder, Fred Ertl Sr., began making toy tractors in his basement. Visit the National Farm Toy Museum to hear how the rest of the story unfolds. Plan to spend a minimum of two hours in this museum.

1110 16th Ave. Ct. SE
563-875-2727
nationalfarmtoymuseum.com

Trip Planning

Dyersville Area Chamber of Commerce

1110 16th Ave. Ct. SE
563-875-2311
dyersville.org

Asian Pho Bistro,
Fairfield Iowa
(Courtesy of Sara Broers)

Index

Swinging Bridge, Iowa Falls
(Courtesy of Michael Broers)